George Brown:
Sprint Superstar

Cliff Brown

Foulis

Haynes

ISBN 0 85429 295 0

© Cliff Brown

First published September 1981

All rights reserved. No part of this book may be reproduced or transmitted in any form or by any means, electronic or mechanical, including photocopying, recording or by any information storage or retrieval system, without permission in writing from the copyright holder.

A FOULIS Motorcycling book

Printed in England by the publishers
Haynes Publishing Group Limited
Sparkford, Yeovil, Somerset BA22 7JJ, England

Distributed in North America by
Haynes Publications Inc
861 Lawrence Drive, Newbury Park, California 91320 USA

Editor: **Jeff Clew**
Cover design: **Phill Jennings**
Layout design: **Rowland Smith**

George Brown, record breaker supreme.

Acknowledgements

I am grateful to Mick Fraser and Jack Lazenby for their help, Vic Willoughby, Peter Davis and *Motor Cycle Weekly* for the use of certain photographs, and *TT Special, Motor Cycle News* and *Motor Cycle Weekly*, who have allowed me to use short extracts from published material.

Especially do I appreciate the interest of the many people who encouraged me to write the book and others who refreshed my fading memory of certain incidents and occasions, including, of course, George's widow, Ada, and son Antony. I want to thank my wife Doreen for her help, and Rosemary Wetherall and Di Davis for typing the finished manuscript.

Even so, the book may not finally have emerged had not Harry Cook, in the early stages, taken the trouble to mention the project to Peter Carrick. I thank particularly, therefore, the former for his interest and the latter for his help, support and, of course, for writing, at my request, the first chapter.

The book is unreservedly dedicated to the memory of George. I can only hope that he would have found it a fitting tribute and that those who so willingly shared a part of his life will take some pleasure, and not a little pride, in reading it.

Cliff Brown,
Stevenage,
Hertfordshire.
January 1981.

Chapter 1

George Brown : Sprinting's Superstar
by Peter Carrick

YOU NEED a lion's heart and a masochistic approach to life to be a motor cycle sprint superstar. There is none of the warm glow enjoyed by the road racer as the vast crowd roars its encouragement; nor the exhilaration and excitement of close combat with others as you open the throttle and with roaring exhaust, wrestle to be out of the hairpin first.

The sprint specialist, by comparison, works in isolation on cold, dismal, windswept airfields. Triumph does not bring a winner's rostrum, a glamour girl to kiss you, or champagne to splash over the crowd. The best you can expect is a quiet 'well done', a friendly thump on the back and a moment of quiet celebration with your small, loyal band of supporters.

Sprinting calls for a special brand of courage, enormous dedication and a commitment to the cause inspired from within. No one in Britain had these qualities in greater abundance than George Brown.

As sprinting's superstar of the 1960s, Brown was a legend in his own time. With the passing years, as he grappled with advancing age and ill-health, he became something of a father figure to a new generation of sprint stars. At the peak of his career he was Britain's fastest motor cyclist and the holder of numerous national and international records.

At 55 Brown was obliged under the rules of the Federation Internationale Motorcycliste to retire from international racing. He didn't like the idea, maintained he was fit enough to continue, and pleaded his case in the most effective and dramatic way he knew: by improving his own standing start sprint solo record by clocking a little under 200 mph.

Four years later, at 59, having made nonsense of the FIM age limit for racers, he set up a new sidecar speed record at 165 mph.

Eventually, even George Brown was forced to acknowledge the passing years and in October 1971 a heart attack signalled the end of his impressive racing career, though his enthusiasm for bikes and record breaking never lapsed. After a period of ill-health he died, suddenly and peacefully, at home in Stevenage, Hertfordshire, in February 1979.

George Brown excelled in many branches of the sport. His passion for motor cycles started while he was at school. By the time he left he had ridden a number of makes, getting his early speed experience riding against the clock around country lanes close to his home at Colwick, Nottinghamshire.

He progressed to trials riding and regularly attended grass-track meetings. His early ambition was to become a solicitor but a move south and a meeting with Philip Vincent changed the course of his life and he accepted the offer of a job at Vincent's small motor cycle factory at Stevenage, where he was soon working in the experimental department. That was in 1934.

At Vincents he did a great deal of high speed testing and his ability to extract the last scrap of energy from an engine became well known. He was keen to go all out racing but his employer refused permission. Not until 1937 was George able to persuade Philip Vincent to let him try. At Brooklands he clocked 113 mph and his 106 mph over two laps of the Outer Circuit was enough to gain him a Gold Star award, though he was not officially entitled to the recognition since he was not a member at the time of the British Motor Cycle Racing Club (Bemsee), whose Gold Star awards were restricted to their own membership.

His early road experience was on a belt driven Raleigh which he shared with brother Cliff. He became very keen on road racing and set off for his first major outing at Cadwell Park. On a Series A Comet Special which he had 'worked on', George won both 500 cc and unlimited events. The crowd was impressed with his performance and would have been even more so had they known that George's victories had followed a nighmarish journey from the south to Lincolnshire during which his competition bike fell from the trailer and into a dyke.

Even after such an encouraging race debut, Philip Vincent still regarded George as being too valuable a member of his technical team to allow him to risk his neck perpetually racing.

After the war, which George spent in the aircraft industry, he returned to road racing in 1947, successfully competing on a Series A Comet Special. George's ability as a road racer was plain and it was an open secret that the famous Joe Craig tried desperately to recruit him for the official Norton team. The prospect was tempting, as was a similar offer from AJS, but George's loyalty to Vincents was even stronger, notwithstanding that the firm was by no means financially sound. Before severing ties with Vincents, however, he and brother Cliff prepared two 500 cc machines for racing. One he rode himself, the other was delegated to John Surtees and both machines were said to be capable of speeds in excess of 120 mph.

It was really George's devotion to Vincent machines and especially the 1000 cc design that led to his parting with Vincent in 1951. George and Cliff had built a prototype machine using conventional suspension and telescopic forks and had proved its superiority; but the factory, committed to an unwavering individualistic policy, refused to follow suit.

So Brown left the firm to open his own motor cycle retail business in Stevenage, literally across the road from the old Vincent works in the High Street in the old town.

His new machine was the forerunner to the first 'Nero' and then the 'Super Nero' which carried him in later years to such fame.

Brown's first outing to the Isle of Man was in 1951 when in the Junior TT he finished fourth on an AJS. In 1952 he competed in the Junior and Senior events, finishing sixth on an AJS in the former and seventh on a 500 cc Joe Potts' Norton in the Senior. It was on the Isle of Man, in 1953, that his road racing career was effectively ended. He came 16th in the Junior event on an AJS but in the Senior race a near tragedy occurred. Charging down Bray Hill he raced into the wreckage of the MV on which Les Graham had been fatally injured. After this incident and sustaining severe facial injuries in crashes at Cadwell Park and Eppynt which he was lucky to survive, George decided to give up road racing to concentrate on hill climbs, sprints, and similar speed events.

The George Brown legend in sprinting was built up around his two famous Vincent-powered machines, the exceptional Nero with a capacity of 994 cc, and the remarkable 1147 cc Super Nero. These were the creations of George Brown and his brother Cliff. They were fitting swinging arm rear suspension and telescopic front forks as early as 1950 and the astonishing reliability of Brown's machines distinguished his performances. In fact during 21 years of competition which brought him numerous FTDs, National and World records, the Vincents only once stopped with engine failure when a piston burned out due to inferior fuel.

At first Nero was intended as a racing machine. Sprinting and hill climbing were only secondary considerations. But it was seldom used for racing, though showed its effective handling numerous times during hill climbs. More specialised preparation was given to Nero in 1960 when sprinting had become much more competitive. Improvements included Avon sprint tyres to give better traction, a longer wheelbase and a lower riding position. Streamlined, but unsupercharged, Nero helped Brown capture his first World record in 1960. That year the machine was timed at 187 mph.

Super Nero was built in 1963 and was identical to its predecessor with a low built rigid frame and a 70 cc Honda front fork. And Super Nero was more powerful, with a supercharged engine.

During his outstanding career, George Brown was a persistent optimist. In 1966, during a four-day Castrol-sponsored record marathon, he made an all-out attempt to become the first man ever to exceed 200 mph on a motor cycle in Britain. But after battling frustratingly against bad weather conditions and on a Greenham Common airfield runway which was unfit for such an ambitious attempt, Brown was denied this ultimate success: though with typical George Brown determination he hung on grimly to the end and on the last day beat or established five National and four World records. It was a sensational achievement.

Best performance was on the 1000 cc supercharged Vincent Super Nero. He broke his own standing-start kilometre record with runs at 18.907 and 19.389 seconds to establish the new time at 19.152 sec. (116.79 mph) against his old record of 19.47 sec. (114.83 mph). The performance also qualified for the British record.

With the same 1000 cc machine, George was only now moving into top gear and he went ahead to establish a World record for the sidecar standing-start quarter-mile at 11.806 seconds ... 76.229 mph.

Until George Brown went to Greenham Common during those October days in 1966, the World record for the sidecar standing-start kilometre was held by Rene Milhoux, on a 1000 cc unblown Vincent at 83.469 mph. George's two runs averaged out at 21.927 sec. giving a record shattering speed of 102.017 mph.

The four-day feast of speed started dismally. Only a few attempts could be made on the first day because of unsuitable weather and most of the time was given to running Brown's 250 cc works Royal Enfield machine. A strong wind prevented him from riding the larger machine seriously, even without streamlining. At the end of the day, only the 250 cc World standing-start quarter-mile had been gained, but the speed was slow against expectation and even George's optimism couldn't see the new record at 60.639 mph lasting very long.

On Thursday spirits sank deeper, rain allowing only a couple of runs on the 250. In spite of the conditions, and irritated by mechanical problems, George managed to ease the record up to 62.15 mph.

Friday's weather was much better and up again went the 250 cc record, this time to 62.630 mph. Then at mid-day, as George was wheeling out the heavier machinery, came drama. The French FIM steward engaged to supervise the record started getting ready to go home that evening. George claimed that the official had been booked for four days — and that included Saturday — the official insisted that his booking ended Friday evening.

Runs were halted while frantic telephone calls were made to Paris, but eventually George won the day and the official agreed to stay over for

Saturday.

George made it all worthwhile, as already reported; but he was by no means finished yet. In spite of a troublesome, gusting wind and an unfortunate dip in the surface of the 2½ mile concrete runway, he wheeled out the 1000 cc Vincent. George said later: *When I came across the dip, going at more than 130 mph when attempting the standing-start kilometre record on the 1000 cc Vincent, the machine bounced 10 feet to the side and I came well off the seat.*

Twice Brown bettered his own World and National standing-start kilometre 1000 cc record, but he was short of the necessary one per cent margin for the runs, described by one observer as 'heroic' in view of the general conditions, to count for new records.

With the runway in such a condition, it would have been foolish for Brown to have gone for his cherished hope of becoming the first man to break through the 200 mph motor cycle barrier on British soil and he was enough of a professional, in spite of his courage, to recognise it. Reluctantly he abandoned any attempt in that direction, consoling himself by attaching a sidecar to the 1000 cc machine. But Friday was not to be Brown's day, mechanical problems preventing runs being made, as they did for attempts with the 1300 cc engine.

In 1964, George Brown, at 51 years old, travelled faster on British soil on a motor cycle than anyone else, clocking more than 195 mph at Chelveston, and he constantly reasserted his ambition to reach that elusive 200 mph.

He pinned his faith in his Super Nero which he and brother Cliff constantly improved. He had many offers for the historic machine, but he refused them all. *I expect it will end up in some museum somewhere,* he once said.

When he recorded a one-way speed of 190 mph he was only 34 mph short of the then existing World record and at the time Brown felt convinced that Super Nero was capable of taking the record. *I was going into the timed quarter at 170 mph and coming out at over 200 mph. The bike was geared for 250 mph, but I was getting savage wheelspin and had to humour the throttle.*

Brown's ambition remained unshakable and in spite of the restricted choice of strips in Britain on which such an attempt could be made, he still felt that there were perhaps a couple of places where it was possible to get the necessary run-in to beat the record.

He chose Greenham Common, as we have seen, and who knows what the result might have been had the condition of the tarmac and the weather been more favourable.

At Elvington in October 1967, he set 171.68 mph for the flying kilometre and 128.7 mph for the standing mile on his famous 1147 cc Super Nero.

Both speeds were easily in excess of the then current World records, but because of the FIM's 55 years age barrier, could only count as British records.

George, in a flurry of defiance, asserted: *I did these runs to show the FIM that their age ban is ludicrous. If I can do that I must be fit,* he remarked. *I am officially fit enough to tackle the British National record with the same machine on Brighton Promenade, where there are railings and lamp standards and all kinds of other hazards, but at Elvington, for instance, which is supposed to be one of the longest and best runways in the country with more than two miles of concrete and tarmac to run on, and on which there are no obstructions, I am not allowed because of my age to make any new World records.*

His runs were outstanding displays of courage, for he rode against the advice of tyre specialists. He had run out of high speed racing tyres and had to depend on a slick back tyre which he considered unsuitable for continuous high speeds. The slicks, predictably, were scuffed badly and one had a long cut in it. Unable to pull up in time at the end of one run, he careered onto the grass and only stopped just short of running completely off the airfield.

George Brown was a credit to motor cycle racing and helped to lift the status of sprinting. In doing so he set almost countless records, urged on by no greater challenge than a stop watch and his own previous best performance. It takes courage, stamina, and tremendous self-will to drive yourself like this from cold to a new record.

Brown's one-man campaign to have the FIM's 55 year old limit on World records dropped was successful and at 56 he responded once again to the self-challenge to be the first man to exceed 200 mph on British soil.

His fastest record at that time was the 189 mph at Chelveston three years before over the flying quarter, achieved with a 'dustbin'-type fairing which at high speed made the front wheel dig into the ground. With a totally enclosed fairing — *I have an expert at the British Aircraft Corporation working on the problem* — the enthusiastic George reckoned he could get just over the 200 mph mark.

Anything faster would be unlikely because of having to pull up at the end of the runway — though airfield runways are the only places in Britain for such attempts, he said.

George Brown was always a racing patriot and he readily confessed that he wanted to crack the record as much for the prestige of Britain as to keep the processes of degeneration at bay. *If I stopped I would feel 56, which I am; but while racing I feel no more than 36,* he once said.

Brown, as recorded earlier, was at Elvington to attempt that elusive 200 mph in October 1968, but luck and weather conditions were against him. But at 58, in 1969, the father of British sprinting was still the fastest two-way motor cyclist in Britain, his 189.33 mph for the solo flying quarter

Chapter 1/13

Waiting for the first light during a record attempt at Chelveston in 1957. *(Motor Cycle Weekly)*

mile and 158.45 mph for the sidecar flying kilometre, still not bettered.

And in September 1970, at The National Sprint Association's pre-records day meeting at Elvington, George roared back into the reckoning for the first time in months, setting fastest speeds in both solo and sidecar classes on the 1000 cc supercharged Vincent Super Nero. In solo form it recorded 176 mph and with sidecar attached, 154 mph.

In 1971, just four months short of his 60th birthday, George Brown's determination and enthusiasm were as high as ever. Although he failed to comply with the regulations required of riders over 55 to submit certificates of fitness from two doctors — *I just didn't seem to get the time to do it this year!* — George said he would go to both The National Sprint Association's and the Incorporated Sprint Organisation's speed weekends and if anyone looked like exceeding his records, he would go out and do something about it anyway.

But only a month later he suffered his first heart attack and the grand old man of British Sprinting had come to the end of the racing road.

After that he lived quietly at his home in Stevenage, content to look back with pride on his numerous records, the last of which he set only a year before at 165 mph when he was 59. Even as late as 1972 he still held a remarkable 13 World and National records and an additional six National-only records.

Now, for the first time, George Brown's story is told in detail by the one person who knew him best and shared the successes and failures of his fast moving career — his brother Clifford, so often the mechanical brains behind George Brown's famous machine. It's an inspiring story which you are certain to enjoy.

Chapter 2

A Time to Remember

GEORGE HADN'T been well for some years and had miraculously survived seven heart attacks. His courage was exceptional. He seemed to ignore advancing age and made few real concessions to it. After being in hospital he was recovering at home and seemed to be making good progress. So when Tony, his elder son who had been taking an increasing part in the family motor cycle repair and retail business in Stevenage, came round to tell me that George had died, I was stunned. It was Tuesday, the date February 27, 1979, and I was sitting quietly at home after my dinner. I couldn't believe it. For a time I sat there and felt chilled, my senses numbed. George, while always vulnerable because of his heart attacks, had seemed so indestructable. My world was shattered. We had shared so much over so many years and all our lives we had been close. I'm not ashamed to say that I just sat there and cried.

We'd never for long been apart. Since kids, we'd camped together; cycled together; motor biked together. And throughout our lives we'd followed one another. Most of all, during all those magnificent days of his racing and record breaking, I had been close at hand, building, preparing and tuning his famous machines. Now he was gone. It was all over. I couldn't believe it.

For a long time I continued to sit there, looking ahead, seeing nothing, but thinking about George. Them, for some unaccountable reason, my mind drifted back, picking at so many wonderful memories. I was back again in 1960 at Thurleigh airfield in Bedfordshire at the time George tackled a number of records including the standing solo kilometre world best. This had stood for quite a number of years to the respected Italian rider Alfredo Milani, father of the famous MV Agusta racer of the 1960s, Gilberto, at 107.84 mph.

These were the early days leading to the peak of George's record breaking career and I remember that back at Stevenage it had been all-out action as we had struggled to get the famous Nero machine ready for the attempts. I had stripped it down and checked and examined everything. We saw the first task as being to crack the World sidecar record held at that time by the legendary 3-wheel specialist Florian Camathias. In those days it was against FIM rules for three-wheeler record attempts to be made with a sidecar passenger, because of the potential danger, and the usual arrangement was to construct what was known as an outrigger which incorporated the third wheel. So George and I set about converting the solo Nero into combination trim. It was necessary for us to build the outrigger for the third wheel and George visited Renolds at Coventry to scrounge some steel tubing. He then made a 12 inch outrigger wheel.

After George had bronzed the three-section frame assembly and we had worked together fitting it to Nero, I made up 35 lb of necessary lead ballast to keep the outrigger stable. This I melted down in a BSA Bantam chaincase, filling the case twice and then bolting the two halves of the hardened lead together. It was then secured to the end of the outrigger near the wheel.

The record attempts were George's idea entirely. He reckoned with Nero he had every chance of bettering the times of both Milani and Camathias and he had shopped around for some very necessary sponsorship. As always in sprinting, money wasn't there just for the asking, but Avon, the tyre specialists, saw the possibility of a reasonable return on their investment if George was successful, particularly as the Motor Cycle Show was to be held shortly afterwards. They pitched in with a generous supply of their new slick tyres. The meeting was to turn out to be quite historic, for it was on this occasion that slick tyres were used for the very first time at a record attempt in Britain, with George the history maker.

It was a wet, bleak and chilly weekend and the isolation of Thurleigh was not at all inviting. Maurice Brierley, a talented sprinter and a close colleague who worked alongside George and myself, was a member of our record-attempt team and it had been agreed that he would have first shot at the kilometre sidecar record with Methamon, his own 1147 cc Vincent outfit. So as George attended to all the airfield formalities Maurice had words with the official timekeepers. Because World records were being attempted, with FIM officials in attendance, the regulations had to be followed exactly and despite the friendliness within our party, there was an atmosphere of strict formality about the proceedings.

It had all been a little eerie as we presented ourselves at the guardroom

Chapter 2/17

at the entrance to Thurleigh. Although the airfield was not being used for everyday flying, only for experimental flights, we had been thoroughly screened by the Air Ministry officials. When we arrived at the guardroom at five o'clock in the morning of Saturday, November 13, 1960, the security guards had a note of all our names and were strict in passing us through.

In the early light Maurice was the first to go, aiming for Camathias' sidecar record of, as far as I can recall, about 96 mph. But the wind was strong and although he made six or seven runs he was repeatedly blown off course, even running out of road and failing to go through the ray trap. During most record attempt weekends there is a constant fight against time and as Maurice seemed to be making little impression, we felt it was time to see what George could do with Nero. He trundled the machine to the start line and as Nero had always been raced solo in the past, we wondered how the third wheel would suit the famous machine. Frankly, both George and I had our doubts because of the necessary flimsy construction of the outrigger. How stable it would be, even with the ballast, was anybody's guess.

Gunga Din and the famous development team in 1949 — (left to right), Cliff Brown, Phil Irving, Mike Egington and George Brown.

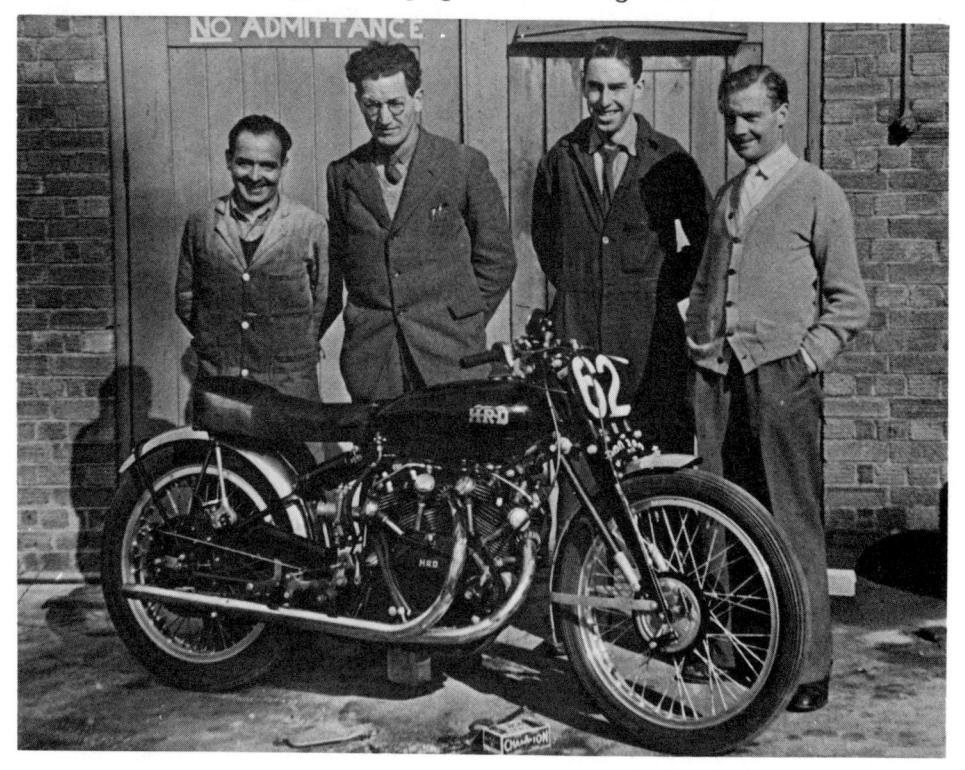

Little by little George nudged the fairing nose forward and with the help of National Sprint Association secretary, Len Cole, eased it to within the regulation 10 cm of the line. A couple of Avon representatives mopped the rainwater off the flat smooth sprint tyre as the timekeepers signalled their okay. With a defiant burst of revs from the exhausts and with the outfit wheels clawing the ground, the unusual looking '3rd wheel'-style Nero rocketed off the mark and disappeared in a cloud of steam as the slicks struggled for adhesion on the wet surface. Clean and sweet came the exhaust note, interrupted only by the growl of three crisp gear changes.

Where Maurice and Methamon failed, George and Nero succeeded, for with two uneventful runs George's average was 98.98 mph (22.6 seconds) and he took the World record by just two miles per hour.

For George one World record was seldom enough, so as the airfield dried out, and with the wind stiffening to around 15 knots, he typically announced he would have a go at the National flying kilometre three-wheeler record. On the first run, he streaked downwind at 143 mph, but with the wind gusting from the left quarter, the return run was much more eventful. No sooner was the outfit within the speed trap than up reared the sidecar to an alarming 45 degrees and George had to fling his body as far as he could to the left — along the sidecar section — to keep it down so that he could hold course. Even so George's speed was 130 mph, giving a new record average of 136.9 mph.

There had already been tremendous excitement, but more was to come as George then decided to go for the standing solo kilometre World record that afternoon. Helped by mechanics Pat Barrett and Tim Hatton of the Stevenage Motor Cycle Club, I dismantled the outrigger assembly from Nero and prepared the machine for its solo run, a much more difficult target this with almost 108 mph being the aim. If George could achieve this, he would take the record by virtue of the FIM's ruling that an existing speed record must be bettered by at least 1 per cent for the new speed to count as a new record. George, though confident, was philosophical about it and although he was keen to go for the record felt that if he didn't make the target, he could wait for a more suitable day.

As one report said: 'The rapid sequence of time-devouring getaways that followed brought a moist gleam to the eyes of the small group of onlookers and gasps of admiration all round.' George was in devastating form, but with a first run at 106.32 mph (21.038 seconds) and a return speed of 105.72 mph (21.156 seconds), his mean time of 106.02 mph was just 0.75 mph short of Milani's record.

Keyed up almost to breaking point, because the track was now becoming very damp indeed, George courageously threw all his long experience and technique into another brace of awe-inspiring runs, but still his effort fell

George showing his race-riding position on Gunga Din.

short. With times of 20.802 seconds and 20.838 seconds his average of 107.44 mph was 0.67 mph better than the World record, but was still 0.04 mph short of the qualifying margin for it to stand as a new World record. His next two runs were even better at 108.06 and 107.24 mph and as we all leaped about and cheered, it looked as if a second World record had been secured over the weekend. But then came savage disappointment. With a couple of quick clips of the throttle before the clutch was released, Nero had apparently edged forward a couple of inches, thereby violating the strict '10 cm from the line' start rule. The A-CU observer had spotted the infringement, but George had propelled Nero from the line before the occial could tell him. George went mad, because at the end of his return run he was convinced he now had the solo record as well. He threw down his gloves and remonstrated with the official, but of course nothing could alter the decision. The runs had already been declared void. He wanted to go again but we talked him out of it because the weather by now was distinctly unfavourable.

It was a desperate disappointment, particularly since I don't believe, until that time, I had seen George perform better at a record-breaking session. We thought about another attempt and although George would have gone again, we all agreed that the track was now too wet and the wind too strong to make a further attempt a serious possibility. We called it a day. George didn't mind too much. He had got close enough to the record to be confident that on another occasion, in better conditions, he could take the record for Britain.

And, curiously enough, he did now hold a rather unusual distinction. For although on a technicality he had failed in his bid to capture the World solo record (all World attempts being under the jurisdiction of the FIM), his sensational final two-way run stood as a new British record, for British records were under the jurisdiction of the Auto-Cycle Union, who weren't given to enforcing the crucial, in George's case, 10 cm start rule. So there was now this remarkable situation: George's new and official British record was better than the current World record. As George said at the time: *Well, it all goes to prove that it's only a matter of time before the World record is mine.*

After it was all over I took Nero down to the fire station at Thurleigh village and stripped it down so that it could be measured and examined by the A-CU and FIM officials. After they had finished their work I re-assembled the engine and we returned to Stevenage, tired but reasonably happy. George had hoisted his name up among the great riders in the record books, with one World record and three British National records. These were George's first major records, but in the undemonstrative world of sprinting, there was no heavy celebration. We called in for a drink at a small village pub on the way home. That's all. I must confess, hardly fitting for a team whose star rider had just secured World and National records. But if there was little time or inclination to celebrate, there was even less time to rest.

The very next day we started cleaning up the bike ready for its presentation at the Motor Cycle Show at London's Earl's Court. Avon's gamble had paid off and their confidence in George and the new and revolutionary slick tyres was rewarded with one of the most exciting exhibits of the entire Show. Nero was given pride of place on the Avon stand where it caused a sensation. Avon had backed the attempt with a good deal of enthusiasm and for their sake we had agreed to keep as quiet as possible about the record breaking weekend. The news of George's success broke at a psychologically ideal moment just prior to the Show and the crowds thronged the Avon stand to see the great machine which was to carve an indelible name for itself in British motor cycle racing history. George was there, pulling in the crowds and signing autographs, and loving every minute of his new found glory: Pat Barrett and myself also spent some time there answering questions about the

The two Georges — Brown (left) and Formby (centre) in 1949, with the famous Vincent machine. *(National Film Agency)*

bike and the record breaking weekend.

It was in the minutes that I sat at home quietly and silently, immediately following the news of George's death, that the events of this spectacular weekend at Thurleigh, for some reason, raced through my mind. The memories were still so vivid, yet it was the most melancholic moment in my life. Even now, more than a year later as I write, I often wake up in the night and think about all the exciting times we had together and what we might have achieved if events had taken a slightly different course. I have no doubt at all that in the 1960s George could have taken the world's outright motor cycle speed record on Super Nero. The bike was fast enough and reliable enough. But while we were able to produce a machine and had the man to beat the rest of the world, we weren't able to persuade anybody to back us. The motor cycle industry didn't want to know and while the giant engineering firm of Rubery Owen to its credit offered us free bits, our essential need was for somebody to pick up our hotel bills and day-to-day expense chitties while we shipped Super Nero and our team across to the Bonneville Salt Flats, and had a serious attempt at the record. But no-one came forward.

Although dear old George achieved so much in his life it was his major disappointment that he wasn't able to bring this ultimate speed title back to Britain. After all, he had done enough to prove the point, for during the time Johnny Allen held the world's fastest crown at 246 mph, George raced Super Nero at Chelveston, one way, at 195 mph unstreamlined, in far from ideal conditions and without any significant sponsorship. Yet how we could expect support at this kind of level when George's outstanding achievements were barely noticed outside the sport of motor cycling. At one time he held 24 World records — a level of success unequalled by any other British motor cyclist — yet he was never honoured at Buckingham Palace, nor was he ever given a civic reception at Stevenage, the town where he lived and worked for so many years and where his famous machines — Gunga Din, Nero and Super Nero — were created.

On that sad day in February 1979, when he died, it was all too late.

Chapter 3

Early Days

WHEELS ALWAYS meant a lot to George and myself and when you know the Brown family background it's not really surprising. Our grandfather owned a successful cycle shop at a place called Pleasley near Mansfield in Nottinghamshire, and for many years made his own models. My father, whom George was named after, was said to have been the first professional chauffeur in the county, driving a well-known local gentleman around in a Beeston car.

When I was 4½ and George about three, we moved from our home in Worksop to Rotherham, my grandfather and father joining forces in a garage business and transporting miners to the pits and back in dilapidated old charabancs. Even our most vivid memories from childhood were about things that moved. I was in the backyard of our Rotherham house one day when an escaped bull charged in and leapt right over me. I can't recall too much about the incident, but the thing that sticks in my mind with uncanny clarity is that I was sitting in my toy motor car at the time. And I continued to sit there, I was later told, despite all the excitement and panic. Another memory from childhood is of a private aeroplane crash-landing in a field near Rotherham. My father managed to buy it from the owner and transferred the engine into a Morgan three-wheeler car he was building. Later, that plane gave George and me a great deal of fun. Even though we were little more than toddlers we took the wings off the crashed plane and spent hours pushing the fuselage up and down father's garage yard. Yes, you could say that the wheels revolution arrived early for George and me.

George was my junior by one year and five months, greeting the world on February 22nd, 1912. Our first home was at Sutton in Ashfield, and we were part of a typical mining community. When my father came out of the Royal Flying Corps in 1918 after war service, he found a job in Nottingham as manager of the Trent Bridge Motor Company. They used to sell Hands and Swift motor cars and also French Beaumont and British Rover motor cycles.

This really was the start of George's life-long obsession with motor cycles. We moved around a lot in those early days as dad tried to get better jobs and I remember when George was little more than 10 that dad bought a side-valve Rover motor cycle and he and his pals used to challenge one another in races along a stretch of public road between Newark and Leicester. George and I used to sit spellbound at home listening to dad recall his deeds and it was this which obviously fired George's enthusiasm for racing and certainly formed the basis of my own mechanical career. I remember dad and a Mr Dowerty sprinting at Clipstone, near Mansfield, a notable venue in those days, on their bikes, a Rover and a Royal Ruby. It was coincidentally the same stretch of road on which the legendary George Brough broke his legs after coming off his motor cycle when a hare ran across the road and the bike hit it. No, sprinting is by no means new. Nor was it new in the 1950s and '60s when George was moving into the big time. Dad and his pals were sprinting as long ago as 1922. The Rover later gave way to extremely fast Douglas which dad used to ride at speed trials.

At one time our family moved into a cottage on an island at Colwick Weir near Radcliffe on Trent, and George and I had to attend school six miles away. The only way of getting off the island was by a swing bridge, so dad bought a motor boat and a rowing boat and us kids had a lot of fun with our new form of transport, boating. They were good, happy days, and although as a family we must have found it tough to make ends meet in those early years after the first world war, there was a kind of foraging satisafaction which was typical of the times as families tried to make their mark.

George had an independent nature and even as a youngster was very self-sufficient. He never intended to worry our parents, but that's not to say that he didn't. The rowing boat dad had acquired used to ship a bit of water and I remember one time George rowing up the River Trent to see a friend. He hadn't returned by ten in the evening and mum and dad were frantic. We decided we must all go in search and started to patrol the river banks, fearing the worst. It was almost midnight . . . and then we heard singing coming from up river and George, totally unconcerned and blissfully at peace with the world, loomed into view. It never occurred to him that his absence might worry or panic the family. He was a typical youngster, full of fun and with unbounded energy. He liked all sports and was football crazy. He was popular at school and a much better scholar than myself.

A natty line in racing attire. George (left) and brother Cliff in 1918.

George and I got on well. There were few brotherly squabbles. George's friends from his later sprinting days will be surprised perhaps to know that at this time, as a youngster of 12, he was a respected member of the local church choir. He had a good voice — and was no dunce at stringing a few words together. He once received a book from the Canadian Government for writing an essay on Canada. I don't exactly remember how it happened, but I do recall that it was quite a big thing at the time and George had to go and have it presented.

I also remember quite clearly those exciting early motor bike rides. Dad had bought a Sparkbrook and he used to let us ride it round the fields and up and down the flood dykes. We fell off plenty of times, but curiously never seemed to hurt ourselves.

At fourteen I left school to become an electrician, but George moved on to Nottingham High School and began to study seriously for a career as a solicitor. This was an almost ashamedly grand ambition for those days, when it was unheard of for children of working class families to consider a professional career. Dad by now was the manager of a local garage, but when this burnt down he looked elsewhere for work and finished up at the Raleigh Company. This meant we had to move again, to a place called Daybrook, close to Nottingham Prison. Dad later bought a fish and chip shop at East Leake, so we moved on yet again. When George and I had time on our hands we used to help out in the fish shop and I remember having to get up at five o'clock in the morning to go to Nottingham fish market, travelling in dad's 3½ hp Raleigh belt drive sidecar combination. One morning we had a puncture in the sidecar wheel and were forced to travel home with the sidecar hoisted high in the air with dad weighting the rear mudguard of the bike so that we wouldn't damage the tyre and tube. Talk about wheelies! Dad was motor bike mad and always tinkering with engines. When he had the fish and chip shop he ran a motor bike workshop as a part-time venture, and even while George was still at school, he and I used to jump at the chance of helping out with all kinds of mechanical jobs.

No matter what the conditions, no matter where we lived, motor cycles always were a big part in our lives. By 1926 when I was sixteen and the General Strike was looming, times were hard and we had moved yet again, this time to Chesterfield where mum and dad took over as licensees of an inn. But we still had the Raleigh belt drive model which I would ride occasionally.

It was not uncommon in those days for youngsters to have their schooling ended prematurely in order to help with the family budget. I'm not sure if this is what happened with George, or that the high school was now too far away for him to travel to every day, but it was while we had the inn that he left school and went to work on a farm. Meantime, dad had exchanged the belt drive Raleigh for a 500 cc saddle tank Raleigh, much more of a 'real' motor bike and although this was an extremely powerful machine, George and I used to ride it quite regularly. I was engine mad by this time and spent hours with dad tuning the machine so that it became very fast indeed. On the way back from a grass track meeting I had been watching, I hit a big hole in the road and came off, making a bit of a mess of the bike. Dad was forced to take it back to Raleigh for repair. When the mechanics took it out on the road for testing after completing the repairs, they were astonished by its speed. They told dad it was the fastest 500 cc bike they had come across and wanted to know what we had done to it.

It was at this time that motor cycle sport really began to take a firm hold of George. The area was a hotbed of activity and clubs from Chesterfield, Derby, Nottingham and Sheffield used to use nearby Holymoorside for their trials competitions. Hungerhill was also used in the International Six Days Trial and George and I had tremendous fun watching both the solo bikes and sidecars.

The inn was not really dad's cup of tea so before long we moved again, this time to London, after dad got a job as manager of a garage at Harrow-on-the-Hill. The garage specialised in the sale of Aston Martin cars and also built P & P motor cycles. I remember both George and I riding the 500 cc

Raleigh with dad on the pillion down to Harrow on the old A1 road when there was hardly any traffic and certainly not a garage for miles so if you broke down you had to do the best you could.

Before long dad left the garage and bought a cycle shop in Harrow and I helped him to do repairs to cycles and motor cycles. Dunelt motor cycles with Sturmey-Archer engines were a good selling line in those days and I remember we once had in the shop window, as a special attraction, the actual Dunelt motor cycle which had won the Maudes Trophy. I can't remember what year that would be, but I'm almost certain the trophy was gained because the bike was ridden round Brooklands for six days and nights without a stop.

George of course was also very involved with the business and we spent much of our time repairing such classic models as the Royal Enfield twins, Calthorpe, Triumph and Raleigh models, and I remember a Humber with an oil-cooled engine. Oil-cooled engines were unusual in those days, but Humber apparently made a few. It was an odd machine to look at; there seemed to be oil all over the engine.

With the shop that dad bought were a number of lock-up garages and some adjacent old sheds, and abandoned in one of the sheds when dad moved in was an old Zenith motor bike, a Gradua gear model with a wicker basketwork sidecar attached. George did a superb job cleaning it all up before applying a coat of varnish, and I concentrated on the engine. When we'd finished it was a source of great pride and provided fun for weeks for the two Brown lads.

I'll never forget taking it out for the first time. As George manoeuvred it with evident pride into the road, with me in the sidecar, we came close to knocking over the law. A policeman had to jump out of the way as the brakes failed to grip on the wet surface; but he wasn't too upset about it. There were fewer restrictions on motor cycles in those days and overall a more charitable attitude towards them and motor cycle riders prevailed. Neither, come to think of it, was insurance necessary!

Even as a teenager George could always get on a strange bike and ride it. He was naturally at home on a bike and it seemed to require no effort on his part, even though he was reasonably small for his age, for him to ride with total control. Dad, who had been a lifetime in motor cycles, always said I was a better rider than George, yet it was I who tended towards falling off. George, after those formative years, never seemed to fall. It wasn't because he didn't go as fast, because most times he travelled faster than I did. Strangely enough I can never remember George or I having a formal lesson on how to ride a motor cycle. It almost seemed to be instinctive, though I suppose there would have had to be times when dad showed us what to do and pointed out the various mechanical parts.

So this was the environment for George and myself during our teens — seldom settled, always caught up in the excitement of transport of one form or another and, of course, because it was the transport of those times, the motor cycle became all-important.

My mother's health suffered while we lived in Harrow and as she was also unsettled there the family decided to move back to Nottingham. Until dad could sell the shop, he and George stayed on in Harrow, while I lived in Nottingham with mother. I got a job with the Raleigh Company as an apprentice and liked it so much I decided to stay, going through the frame and engine assembly departments. I also spent some time servicing bikes. It was here I had my first experience of road testing. Even now, at close on 70, I'm only 5'2" tall and back in those days might even have been smaller, so I fitted well onto the tiny 2¼ and 2½ hp side valve models, I later took over the testing of 250, 350 and 500 cc Raleighs with an old school pal called Harold Pycroft. Harold was second in charge to Wilf Joseph who then used to ride at Nottingham speedway with his pal Bill Varly, on a Norton-engined dirt bike.

Part of that early environment. George and Cliff's mother outside the shop at Harrow-on-the-Hill in 1928.

Raleigh was, of course, one of the big names in motor cycling in the 1920s and early 1930s. Established as early as 1899, specialising in the manufacture of both pedal cycles and motor cycles they, like other factories at that time, tried to capitalise on the trend to motor bikes. For a time they were highly successful, producing a number of high quality models including a 798 cc V twin, a 500 cc flat twin, and other 350 cc, 500 cc and 600 cc models. But the depression of the 1930s brought a significant fall-off in their motor cycle sales. My father later worked at Raleigh in the Experimental Department and also serviced Sir Harold Bowden's Rolls-Royce — a rare honour in those days because there weren't too many Rolls-Royce cars about in Nottingham, or anywhere else for that matter. Sir Harold was the owner of Raleigh at that time, his father starting the business in an old shed on the very site the highly successful company of today occupies.

I was earning good money working at Raleigh so I discarded the old bike which had given me such good service for a side-valve 250 cc AJS. George later inherited this bike and it gave excellent service as he rode it to and from work.

With some of the cash I was now earning I was able to buy dad a Morris Minor overhead camshaft car so that he could sell off his faithful old bull-nosed Morris. On the Minor, George, myself and dad polished the head out and made a 2 inch diameter exhaust pipe for it. These were the days before it was realised that big exhaust pipes could make a difference to performance. A 3 inch diameter pipe hadn't been heard of then. It was purely an experimental idea of dad's, but it worked well and the car was capable of between 70 and 75 mph without any bother. These were interesting days, looking back. I met Jack Williams while working for Raleigh. He rode the legendary D.R. Donovan's outside flywheel Raleigh and I had the honour of being the only mechanic to test ride the production 250 cc camshaft-engined Dunelt. This remarkable model had an engine designed by F. Vines and a frame designed by T.L. Williams, the bike being assembled at Raleigh. I think it was at that time the only 250 cc camshaft engine being built.

In the 1930s, when the big slump came, George and I were in our twenties. George managed to get a job driving a lorry for a garage near Nottingham, taking gravel to a Borstal which was being built nearby. He also worked for Raleigh, driving an articulated lorry loaded with bikes to the Liverpool docks. I remember he once got the truck stuck under a low-level bridge and some of the top crates in which the bikes were packed, crashed down onto the road, smashing quite a number of the bikes. It was an insurance job and George was very upset. He was afraid of losing his job. Although he had enormous courage when racing or record breaking, he was quite sensitive in situations where he felt he might have let someone down or had fallen down on his responsibilities.

Raleigh's motor cycle sales dropped and in a gambling effort to diversify, they decided to make a three-wheeler van, with the single wheel up front. In the light of today's advanced technology it must appear crude and speculative in the extreme, but by the standards of the day nobody considered it unusual for this new vehicle to embody the frame of a 600 cc Raleigh with the same forks and front wheel attached to the chassis. The Sturmey Archer engine and gearbox were chain driven to the back axle. It was difficult to decide whether you drove or rode the van! You certainly sat astride with the tank between your knees, using handlebars to steer. But you had to keep the steering damper on. You got into terrible wobbles if you didn't!

Nowadays, of course, such monstrosities would be banned without comment or dissent, but in the early 1930s this kind of vehicle was a fairly common sight. They were popular as bread delivery vans and used by ice cream salesmen. A development of the van was a Raleigh three-wheeler car called the Safety Seven. I still have a spares book of this model and the small tool box I used to carry with me in case I broke down while out testing.

Work schedules in those days were prodigious and when times got hard and there was no testing to be done, we used to fill in by delivering vans and cars all over the country. Job specification didn't count for much then. On one occasion I remember going off to deliver a van to Shrewsbury from Nottingham and not getting back for three days! When I arrived at Shrewsbury they had another van ready for me which was needed in Bristol. So on I went. In Bristol they asked me to deliver another van to Minehead and from there I returned to Nottingham with a service van. Nobody had thought about expenses and, not surprisingly, I ran out of cash, spent one night sleeping in the van near Bristol Zoo, and had to cable Raleigh for money to keep me going in food and lodgings.

They were stirring times though and we managed to cram in a good deal of fun. George and I, along with a gang of enthusiasts, used to go to early race meetings at Castle Donington and have bets between us on who would win. One Saturday I won almost £5 on an Alfa Romeo driven by an unkown called Richard Shuttleworth. He later became famous for his aeroplane collection at Old Warden, near Biggleswade in Bedfordshire. Another brush with fame came while I was testing a van chassis. I pulled up at the side of the road near Beeston to make an adjustment when a man in RAF uniform drew up on a Brough Superior and asked if I was all right. We had a pleasant chat, got on well, and after a time I told him my name was Buster Brown (my workmates' name for me because of my obsession with motor bikes). He said he was Aircraftman Shaw and I was shattered to learn much later that he was the famous Lawrence of Arabia. I used to see him quite a lot after that meeting and we would talk at length about motor cycles and, in particular, his favourite Brough Superior. He was an extremely pleasant man and I was shocked to learn later than he had been killed while riding his beloved motor cycle.

It was shortly after this that I crashed into a lorry almost directly outside the Raleigh main gate and had my right ear almost severed by flying glass. I was rushed to hospital where the flopping ear was sewn back on. The doctors did such a wonderful job that even today you can't see the join! They say how wonderful this kind of surgery is now, but fifty years ago it was a miracle.

Dad had the wanderlust again and after landing a garage manager's job in Walthamstow, he, my mother and George moved once more. I still had a job at Raleigh and decided to stay in Nottingham finding lodgings at Burton Joyce. Shortly after, the recession began to bite more deeply and about 1933, I think it was, Raleigh decided to stop making motor cycles and three-wheelers in order to concentrate on pedal power. It wasn't really surprising. In the 1926 strike Raleigh's stockrooms had been chock-a-block with motor bikes, but they could still sell push bikes. Another major disincentive to motor cycle production in those days was that all models went back to the factory for repair, not to the dealer. Even crashes. Most of the motor cycle testers from Raleigh went to work for Rolls-Royce at Derby, but that kind of move didn't appeal to me. As the shutters began to go up, Harold Pycroft and I bought the last two 350 cc Model G Raleighs with upswept pipes to be made, paying £25 each for them, and rode down to the Motor Cycle Show in London. Back in Nottingham, Harold, too, decided then to go to Rolls-Royce. After testing the last of the cars, vans and motor cycles to be manufactured at the factory, I turned down a job in the cycle department.

Meantime, T.L. Williams, the works manager at Raleigh, and Raleigh's former general foreman, Hewitt Thompson, had decided they might be able to salvage something for themselves out of the Raleigh ruins and were determined to carry on making the three-wheeler vans from an old mill they rented at Fazeley on the A5 near Tamworth. Just before leaving Raleigh for the last time I got a telegram from 'T.L.' asking me to go to Tamworth to see him about a job. When I got there, it was like a Raleigh reunion. Bill Taylor, Raleigh's motor cycle assembly foreman, was already there, along with a number of apprentices from Nottingham and I decided to take on the job as tester. It was Bill Taylor, myself and the apprentices who built the first van at Tamworth under the trade name Reliant, which was of course to become well respected later. The firm also became famous as manufacturers of the Scimitar and Robin vehicles. The Reliant was virtually a copy of the Raleigh model with a 600 cc side valve JAP engine and handlebars for steering. These vehicles were hand made by about a dozen people and although the model showed a lot of promise, sales were never good enough to keep us busy for more than half a week. So we worked for maybe three days and collected dole money for the remainder of the week. What kept Reliants going was their inheritance of all the one-time Raleigh agents, since there was no other three-wheeler available to take the place of the Raleigh model.

For a time George and I didn't see all that much of one another. I had worked for Raleigh and then Reliant, but I knew that his interest in motor cycles had been developing rapidly and that he had gone to work for the Vincent motor cycle factory in Stevenage, Hertfordshire. But the time was fast approaching when our lives would be closely intertwined and the process began when mother decided once again that she didn't like London and moved with George to Baldock, some 35 miles north, in Hertfordshire. Baldock was chosen because mother had relatives there. George moved with her while dad used to travel home to them at weekends, keeping the Walthamstow garage going during the week.

George had been working with dad in the garage, but moving to Baldock made him look for a job nearer his new home. One day the man who was to become the most famous sprinter of his time in the world and certainly the most notable employee for many years at Vincent HRD, presented himself at Vincent's works at nearby Stevenage and asked for a job. They set him to work in the service department where he was kept busy repairing the second-hand bikes which were taken in part exchange against new Vincents. That was in 1933. Things, meantime, were growing desperate at Reliants and after visiting my mother at Baldock with my wife of six months, I also decided to enquire about a job at Vincents — known then simply as HRD. I was poking around the showroom, which is now part of the Aleynes Grammar School, when Mr Vincent came and asked me if I wanted to buy a bike. I told him I was just looking around. Then I took my courage in both hands and told him: well, I'm looking for a job. I told him of my experience with Raleigh, that George was already employed there, and that I had worked with motor cycles all my life. After an interview with Mr Frank Walker, who was the managing director, I was taken on as a fitter. That was in August 1934 and although the war would eventually come along to interrupt things, it was the beginning of those glorious days of Vincent HRD. More than that even, it was the start of the close association between George and myself which was to remain virtually intact until his death more than 40 years later and which would witness the emergence of George, first as a trials rider, then a worthy hill climber and road racer, and lastly as a remarkably successful sprinter.

Chapter 4

The Vincent Days...and Gunga Din

GEORGE WAS 22 when he joined the Vincent factory in 1934. Curiously enough it was known to everyone locally as the HRD factory, though the imposing figure of Philip Vincent was very much in evidence on a daily basis and no-one was left in doubt who was the boss. Not that he wielded the big stick. A quiet air of authority was more his style and he was well liked and respected by the workforce. Everyone generally agreed that it was a good firm to work for and if you knew your job and got on with it, they left things to you.

My first job there was polishing bronze and cast iron heads and fitting the working parts to the heads. Pay was 9 old pence an hour and as much overtime — at the same rate! — as I wanted. George was on about the same money and after starting in the service department, was soon promoted to the test and special bike department. He was very impressed when he discovered that a workmate called Peter McIver used to race at Brooklands. George was a good and conscientious worker and got on well. In fact those early days at the Stevenage works were very happy. The firm had been established only for about five years and Mr Vincent had a lot of ambition. A century before, the Stevenage premises had been occupied by a well respected firm of carriage builders, who had long since moved to London. Before Philip Vincent found them empty they had been used as a brewery and George, myself and a lot of the lads worked in what had been the old malt sheds. When George and I joined, there were about 30 of us all told in the company. We all pulled the same way and there was a kind of adventure and crusade about the whole thing. On average we would produce some seven machines a week — Comets, Comet Specials and Meteors.

To fill in the background, Philip Vincent was a motor cycle youngster who had gone to Cambridge University to read Mechanical Sciences at Kings College. He already had an ambition to be a motor cycle manufacturer and while at Cambridge got his father to finance the building of a prototype motor cycle he had designed. The design was encouraging and the young and ambitious Vincent asked for more financial backing to start his own company. This was forthcoming, subject to some judicious monitoring of the project by one of Vincent Senior's business associates, and suitable premises were found at Stevenage. By this time HRD Motors Ltd had been acquired by Bill Humphries of OK Supreme, but Philip Vincent was able to buy the name and goodwill for a modest price, forming the Vincent HRD Company Ltd in 1929.

A mass production operation was never intended. Howard Davies had built up a firm reputation as head of HRD for producing quality machines of distinction. Vincent continued this policy and the first bikes by the Stevenage concern bore the old HRD tank emblem. At this time 500 cc JAP and Rudge engines were bought in for fitting into the frames, although Phil Irving, the brilliant engineer from Australia, had already joined the company and was hard at work on a Vincent engine. Philip Vincent had already done enough to achieve immortality in the motor cycle world with the introduction of his famous cantilever spring frame. Prejudice against rear springing, claimed as potentially dangerous, was rife and virulent in those days. It makes me smile to think that 40 years later the Japanese were claiming their cantilever frame as — 'A new idea'!

George had settled down as well and as quickly as I was to do later. The testing and sporting element captured his interest and he was well satisfied with the racing plans Vincent had for his machines, though they were, of course, production models, not out-and-out racers. Nonetheless the new company had inherited a proud racing tradition, for HRD himself had won the Senior TT and finished second in the Junior race on machines of his own manufacture in 1925. Two years later Freddie Dixon on an HRD machine won the Junior TT — and in 1934, when George and I joined the firm, a director of the company, Captain Bill Clark, rode a Vincent HRD machine, equipped with a new Vincent engine, to win a gold medal with no points lost in the 1934/35 International Six-Days Trial.

George was already hooked on speed riding and being a tester gave him all the opportunities he wanted at that time. The roads around Stevenage became the background to a 'cat and mouse' existence with the local police who, understanding though undoubtedly they were, couldn't really be expected to turn their blind eye in George's direction when he consistently reached speeds well in excess of 100 mph on roads which carried pre-war traffic averaging between 40 and 50 mph.

Just three incidents I knew about at the time will serve to indicate George's enthusiasm for the job and his growing relish for a life of speed. Testing motor bikes on the open road with the local police station only about a half mile from the factory gates was too much of a challenge, even for George, so he would ride sedately up to the nearby open stretch of Letchworth Gate before opening the throttle. Not surprisingly, he would sooner or later be reported to the police for speeding and, as George told me and we all knew well enough at the factory, he would catch sight of the police and make a dash for home with the law in hot pursuit. From that point on the routine was well established. Back at the works everything would be calm and we would be getting on normally with our jobs when suddenly George would race into the yard, drive round out of sight and, with great urgency and with hardly a word, would immediately lock the machine away in one of the sheds. When the police arrived some minutes later, they would find George working away innocently on a stone cold machine. They were really very understanding, but having had the incident reported to them, they naturally felt it their duty to follow it through.

Once, at least, George pushed them too far and the police felt disposed to take real action. They were waiting for him as he rushed through a nearby village early one morning. He was caught, had no excuse to offer, and was subsequently charged with speeding. In court at Hitchin the magistrate enquired George's speed at the time. The policeman replied: *'One hundred and ten miles an hour'* and said his stop watch confirmed it. The magistrate simply couldn't believe it and dismissed the case . . . much to George's amusement.

So irrepressible was George in those days that when the police finally took the only action possible and put up 30 mph signs along George's 'test strip', they were mysteriously uprooted and deposited in the garden of the police station two or three times before George felt the point had been made and gave in gracefully.

Unknown to the Vincent hierarchy, George would also take out the second-hand 'repair jobs' that came into the factory and thoroughly enjoy himself under the guise of 'test runs': and he, Harry Swain and George Eastham constantly challenged one another to see who could get from the Vincent factory to nearby Walkern village, some four or five miles away, in the shortest time. I think the time eventually got down to about three minutes.

More and more George was spending his time testing machines and his dedication and loyalty to Vincent was outstanding. This would be put to the test sometime after George returned to the Stevenage factory at the end of the war. He was at that time riding privately for Joe Potts, the noted North of England sponsor, when Norton approached him about a TT ride. Their rider Rod Coleman had crashed and broken a collar bone and the illustrious Norton race team management wanted George to take over. But he was so loyal to Vincent that he turned them down. They switched then to their second choice, George's rejection significantly providing the opening for a young talented rider called John Surtees!

In 1951 AJS wanted George to ride for them, but again his loyalty to Vincent over-rode his personal racing ambitions and he stayed with the Stevenage factory. But in the meantime he was kept fully occupied and at weekends rode Vincent machines in numerous road races and competed in trials on his own machine.

Vincents competed in the TTs for the first time in 1934 with three riders, Jack Williams, Arthur Tyler and John Carr, but after a few quick laps with Jack Williams turning in an average lap speed in excess of 70 mph all three machines, which were fitted with JAP engines, failed. By 1936, however, the Comet engine had been designed by Phil Irving and it was the responsibility of Bill Ling, the chargehand in the engine assembly department, and myself, to build the Comet specials for the Isle of Man before they went to the special department for superchargers to be fitted by George and Peter McIver. On the brake test they proved satisfactory, so the new engines were fitted into the special frames by Ted Hampshire and sent to the Isle of Man. But on the island the engines did not prove themselves because of the altitude, so the blowers were taken off and the bikes ridden as conventional machines with atmospheric induction. Really, Vincents didn't have enough knowledge and experience of jet sizes at that time. I remember George riding one of the machines at speed on the island . . . testing it over the mountain mile without a crash helmet!

It was around this time that Mr Vincent decided to open up a showroom in Chesterfield so that enthusiasts further north did not have to travel to Stevenage to buy his motor cycles and George did a stint up there as temporary sales manager. When he came back, Mr Vincent and Mr Irving had decided to design and make a 1000 cc twin which Bill Ling and I used to call the plumber's nightmare because it seemed to have pipes all over it. There was a fair bit of skill required in building the engine. Timing the valves of the rear cylinder was easy, but when it came to the front cylinder, you had to keep taking the cam out, undoing four nuts in the process, and turning the cam wheel round in slots until it was right for the rear one. Once you got the hang of it, it was all right, and of course this was before the machine went into production. If my memory serves me well the first 1000 cc Vincent to be built was DUR 142, which was used first as a factory runabout, but later George rode it at Brooklands at an average speed of 113 mph in the rain. George was also at this time proving a very capable rider at grass track meetings on a 350 cc Velocette.

They were exciting, exhilarating days, but soon they were to be rudely interrupted as Europe plunged into war. As Vincents dismantled their bike production facilities and prepared for wartime manufacture, George went off to work for Percival Aircraft at Luton, who had started building Mosquitos, as an assembly foreman. He also got me a job there but Philip Vincent wouldn't let me go and I spent the war in Stevenage as an aircraft parts inspector at the Vincent factory. George wanted desperately to get into the RAF and volunteered a number of times. But with Percival Aircraft he was in a reserved occupation and they wouldn't let him go. But with the war over in 1945, the Vincent factory was still there when George and I were able to get back to a more normal life, and George couldn't return to the world of motor cycles quickly enough.

While still working at Percival Aircraft he quickly got involved again with Vincent in his spare time and it was always his intention, once he was released from his war work, to go back to the Vincent factory. When George married in 1946, it was to a North Country lass whose family had moved down to live in Stevenage.

There was already a lot going on at Vincents. During the winter of 1944/45, Mr Vincent and Mr Irving had done some preliminary design work on what was a Series B Rapide. I felt privileged to be the only person other than draughtsmen Bob Kinolty and Matt Wright, and Mr Vincent and Mr Irving, of course, to see the early plans. Mr Vincent's office had been turned into a temporary design room and I still remember very vividly Mr Vincent calling me in to have a look at the drawings. With the war over, I was instructed to clear out the old carpenters' shed and told to prepare to build some twin flywheels — 30 sets altogether — for when the crankcases were finished.

An early fall at the hairpin at Cadwell Park in 1946. George got up and continued the race. *(George Schofield)*

I fitted the first set to the first prototype Rapide B on January 12, 1946, and built the engine complete, myself, except for the cams which were bought in from Weyburn Engineering. Most of the components were experimental, though the frame was built on the same lines as the sloper Panther, but featuring a front tube frame.

George couldn't wait to get his hands on the machine and spent almost all his spare time down at the factory. But first Graham Walker and Arthur Bourne, the then editors respectively of *The Motor Cycle* and *Motor Cycling*, were given the opportunity to test the machine. Arthur Bourne thought the road holding was magnificent and, although a 1000 cc, he reckoned it behaved as sensitively as a 500 cc in traffic. Graham Walker was likewise much impressed by the design, the compact nature of the machine, and its handling. The bike was road tested from about April to September 1946 and after Mr Vincent, Mr Irving and Matt Wright, who designed the New Imperial cross-flow cylinder head, had ironed out a few minor teething problems, it turned out to be a very good machine indeed.

These immediate postwar years were grim. The big freeze and power cuts of 1946/47 led the country into a shortened work week and to rationalise things, we combined Vincent's two factory units. I remember us on an earlier occasion using 10 gallon oil drums for coke fires to keep warm. Those were the days! But business was brisk and soon I had to employ more men to build engines and to do small assembly fittings. Then Mr Irving asked me if I would like to work in the development department permanently, and I jumped at the chance, leaving Dennis Minett in charge of engine assembly.

This led to the building of the second B Rapide and at about 10,000 miles the solo machine was converted to sidecar trim with 3 inch top fork links, 180 lb fork spring, sidecar rear frame springs and a 56 tooth rear sprocket. A Miller sidecar body was used on a converted Noxal chassis and if I remember correctly, George rode the bike in the Lands End trial with Stan Applebee in the sidecar and won a 3rd class award. Mr Irving later took the bike to the Isle of Man where it was entered by Vincent's Blackpool agents, Fairburns, in the Clubmans TT.

In the winter of 1946/47 George, along with service foreman Norman Brewster, approached Mr Vincent about building a Series A Comet Special for short circuit racing as an interim measure while a new Vincent 500 cc model was prepared. He somewhat grudgingly gave his consent, provided George and the rest of us could find sufficient parts lying around. The three of us turned out the sheds and were lucky because we literally found everything we needed in the TTC17 Comet Special engine and frame which Captain Clark, a top man at Vincents, had ridden and raced at Donington. George and Norman worked like Trojans on the frame assembly while my job was to strip down the engine and rebuild it with a new big end. It

At Dunholme in 1947 with George somewhere in the pack. *(George Schofield)*

looked as good as new when finished and by skilful drilling and lightening George managed to get the weight of the original 1938 engine down from well over 300 lb to 290 lb.

It turned out to be a very successful machine. Its first outing was at Cadwell Park which, following the demise of Brooklands, became the main place for racing on the mainland. It was at Cadwell that George competed for the handsome silver Folbigg Trophy and on this machine won it three or four times in all. So what more natural than that it should be dubbed the Cadwell Special. The bike was still in existence into the 1980s and was ridden regularly at Mallory Park and elsewhere in the races held for vintage machines.

It was all very hard work, but rewarding and good fun. I remember George and myself on our way to Cadwell one time, me leading the way riding the Vincent development sidecar and George, with his friend Bob Slater, following along driving his MG sports car with the Cadwell race bike mounted on the attached trailer.

Many of the roads in the Boston area in those days had deep dykes alongside and all at once I lost sight of the MG. I turned round and went back in search and found the trailer and bike deep in the roadside ditch. The trailer had broken loose and it was fortunate that no serious damage had been done to the machine. We hitched a tow rope to the trailer and managed to haul everything back onto the road. I should mention that it was by now four o'clock . . . *in the morning.* We took the bike from the trailer, turned it upside down to drain the water from the engine, put petrol in the tank, and with two or three stout pushes down the road, the bike fired and George raced it up and down to dry out the engine. The bike was of course in race trim, with no baffles and devoid of silencer and, because of the open pipe, it made a tremendous racket. At that time in the morning it must have been heard as far away as the centre of Boston.

We never discovered how the news had got around, but when we arrived at Cadwell Park everybody appeared to know about our escapade. In spite of everything George had a magnificent day, winning every race he entered . . . with a drying out engine!

George loved the Cadwell Special and was very upset once when Dennis Minett borrowed it for a race on the Continent, came off and badly damaged it. We literally had to rebuild it before George could take off again.

By this time George had left Percival Aircraft and was working full time at Vincents as a special bike tester and was also racing for them. He was also a member, along with Mr Vincent and myself, of the development department. It was just what George wanted and he relished the long hours and the exciting times. There was a lot going on. One interesting project developed after Mr Irving had been approached by West Ham Speedway to make a speedway engine like the TT17 Cadwell engine. But the boss went one better, he and Philip Irving designing an engine which utilised a Rapide cylinder head and barrel and a Series A motor. It was quite an assembly job! We started by sawing all the fins from the barrel and cylinder head so that the engine would warm up quicker, a vital need in a speedway engine. The first engine had a special Elektron crankcase into which we drilled and tapped two holes in the drive and timing side cases, to be fitted with screw plugs which could be taken out so that we could plug the flywheels (which were also drilled and tapped) for balancing. I spent a day at West Ham speedway track with Matt Wright, as Malcolm Craven, his machine fitted with the new engine, rode round and round the track until we had cured the vibration. Malcolm Craven had a couple of engines which he used during the entire season. They never let him down and I only had to replace broken valve springs. Eric Chitty, the West Ham captian, also had one on loan. After the speedway engine had gone so well, George scrapped the original unit in the Cadwell Special — which was later used successfully in hill climbing — and

Up a 1 in 2½ at Cadwell in 1948.

Hero of the day. On the Cadwell Special George won five races at Scarborough. *(George Schofield)*

used the speedway engine, with necessary modifications. Overall George was practically unbeatable with his Cadwell or Speedway Special, though sadly the speedway engine was never a commercial success.

George always took his racing seriously and used to keep fit by riding in trials on an ex-army Matchless, on which he twice won the BHN group trial. Both George and I had put in long hours working on the Cadwell bike, George concentrating on the frame and general assembly, with myself the expert on the engine, keeping it well tuned. We used to stay late at the factory, working well into the night on a number of days every week. It was a very committed time.

It was while we were racing the Cadwell bike that Mr Irving decided he wanted a standard Rapide making into a racer. We found a production engine which was a throw-out from road test — number F10AB/1A/71.1 to be exact, because I have a note of it to this day! — and while George again concentrated on modifying the frame (this time with Mr Irving himself) and wheels by drilling for lightening, I dismantled the engine, checked all the parts, tuned the cylinder heads to a highly polished finish, together with the inside of the crankcase, and then I picked out some good cams for identical timing 80/82 degrees overlap. It was also fitted with low compression pistons, because of the low quality fuel then available. I cleaned all the parts, reassembled the engine, and did everything I could to make the oil run smoothly — polished the rockers and conrods which were of 65 tons tensile steel, lightened and polished the flywheels, fitted extra inner valve springs and made bronze adaptors for 1 1/8 inch carbs. A standard Lucas KVF mag with auto-advance was used and when the bike was finished it looked like a real racer.

George took the machine out for a run one evening on trade plates to see how it handled and he said it felt like a dream. I think George rode it to win the unlimited class at the 1947 Cadwell meeting and at Abridge in Essex; the bike was so fast that George had it running well ahead of Johnny Lockett on a works Norton (would you believe!) until the last lap when the gearbox seized and threw him off. George and I were hardly worth living with when I discovered that one of the apprentices had not put enough oil in the gearbox. After that no-one ever touched one of George's racing bikes but me.

George's next major race was the classic Hutchinson 100 at Dunholme aerodrome in October 1947. We assembled the engine with higher compression pistons, intermediate ratio gear fitted G9/1 and G11/2 and the short teeth in G11/2, G6 and G13, ground away to give some backlash on second and bottom gears. The front carb was fitted with a mixing chamber sloping inwards and a 15 degree down-draught float chamber. We also fitted it with separate 1 5/8 inch diameter, 54 inch long exhaust pipes and added an extra 1¼ gallon compartment to the petrol tank to give as much uninterrupted running as possible, an advantage in such a long race.

I rode the bike up to Mansfield on trade plates and the next day George did magnificently by finishing second to Ted Frend on one of the AJS Porcupine racing twins. He led the unlimited class for the first lap. Ted's race average was 87.17 mph, George's 85.04 mph, though it must be remembered that the Vincent Rapide was basically a standard model. But it showed what it could become with careful engine building.

It was this machine which became the famous Gunga Din, so christened shortly after the Hutchinson meeting by Charles Markham, who took it out on road test for *Motor Cycling*. He was extremely impressed by its performance and the name was extracted from Kipling's popular phrase of the time *... you're a better man than I am, Gunga Din.*

George was doing a lot of testing at this time and his speeds on various Vincent specials were most impressive. For instance, I remember him doing substantially in excess of 125 mph at Gransden airfield with an original Vincent TTC engine which I had dismantled and reassembled to Black Shadow specification because Mr Vincent and Mr Irving wanted a faster machine for record breaking on the continent.

Showing neat racing style at Cadwell Park in 1947 on the HRD TT Replica.

At this time George was turning in some extremely creditable performances, both on the Cadwell bike and Gunga Din, and just before the 1948 TT I remember that at Haddenham in Buckinghamshire he won every race he entered on the Cadwell bike. And this was against some really top-line professional racing opposition in the form of Nortons, AJSs and Triumphs ridden by Geoff Duke, Bill Doran, Ted Frend, Syd Barnett and the Australian Harry Hinton. George's repeated wins rattled some of the other competitors so much that complaints were received by the officials that he had entered Gunga Din for the meeting, but so far had not ridden it. They scathingly suggested he was afraid to ride it and said he should be made to bring it out.

They were desperate to separate George from his winning Cadwell bike by some means or other and there was a certain degree of scepticism about the 1000 cc Gunga Din. The Cadwell bike weighed some 290 lb while Gunga tipped the scales at a mighty 400 lb. I remember Mr Irving coming over to George and me in a raving temper over what the others had been saying and instructing George to take out the bike in the very next race and show them that it could be ridden, in spite of its weight. George took up the challenge and was into the first bend almost before some of the others had started. He won the race handsomely and broke the course record for the meeting. Later the meeting officials ran an invitation race, but George, still annoyed about the unsporting attitude of some of the other riders, refused to take part.

It was in 1948 that George raced for the first time on the Isle of Man, in the Clubman's TT. By this time the factory had sold enough Vincent Rapides for Mr Vincent to decide that George and Phil Heath should ride them on the Island and after working hard on a couple of engines which had been rejected in road tests as bad rattlers, I was happy when George got away to a good start and was leading the race with a nine second margin on the first lap. In practice he had deliberately kept his times down to fool the opposition and to avoid any possibility of blowing up the engine.

In the race he was in tremendous form. He covered the first lap in just 28 mins 19 secs at an average of 80.39 mph and did even better second time round, pushing his speed to 80.51 mph. He was well in the lead as he pulled into the pits for refuelling. As the nozzle of the fuel pipe was pushed into the tank aperture, George grabbed a clean pair of goggles, threw away the old, fly-bespattered ones, and without hesitation kicked the bike back into life. He roared away and disappeared over the brow of Bray Hill. He was still in front at the end of lap three, which he completed at an even faster pace, flashing past the pits at around 115 mph, and now he looked to be a certain winner.

But only twenty minutes later, with George going like the wind, the

Vincent mysteriously faltered, spluttered and finally died. George couldn't believe it. He checked the machine. Everything seemed in order. He pulled open the fuel filler cap and to his horror found the tank . . . bone dry.

With some six miles still to go the task was daunting and no-one would have blamed him for admitting defeat there and then. Instead he started pushing the big machine, which in touring trim weighed 460 lb. Luckily, much of the distance was downhill, but there was the formidable climb up from Governor's Bridge to come and then the long, wearying and seemingly never-ending straight to the pits. He coasted downhill, lying on the tank to reduce wind resistance and conserve his energies. Panting and sweating, he peeled off items of race-wear to gain relief from the strain. His muscles aching with the effort, he was subjected to the demoralising experience of rivals racing past to finish ahead of him, But he pushed on, only to stop short of the finishing line to scramble back into his jerkin, and put his gloves, goggles and helmet back on, since the rules demanded that riders finish the race fully clothed or be eliminated from the results.

It was a superhuman effort and as he stumbled past the timing box, panting, sweating and struggling, he received a hero's acclaim and a bigger cheer than that given to the winner, John Daniels. He was almost on the point of collapse as his wife Ada greeted him and supported him to the ambulance tent. Despite everything, he finished in a creditable sixth place.

George was disconsolate, for his outstanding ride would otherwise almost certainly have given him victory at his first attempt in the Clubmans, and not too many riders achieve that. Knowing George as I did, I knew just how low he must have been feeling, but once he recovered his comment was typical of the man: *Another half-pint of petrol and I should have been home,* was all he said. Although he was a novice at TT racing he showed as much pluck as the most experienced Mountain rider and did come away with the consolation of having raced the fastest lap at 82.65 mph and therefore collected the Dunlop Trophy.

George's wife, Ada, called by the officials to the finishing straight so she would be there to greet her husband in triumph, was forced to wait helplessly for 39 minutes as he struggled to complete the gruelling tramp to the line. *I could hardly stop myself from rushing out and helping him,* she said; while dad just stood there and wept openly.

George's time for the entire race, including pushing the last six miles, was an impressive 2 hours 3 mins 18 secs (73.48 mph). Ted Davis in fifth position had taken 2 hours 1 min 44 secs, so it's easy to appreciate the commanding position George held on the leaderboard until he ran out of fuel.

It was also in 1948 that George had his first serious crash. But before that he won the 50-mile race at Scarborough to collect his fifth cup and by then had set new records at numerous courses with Gunga and the Cadwell

Special. Among the more unusual perhaps was the sand record standing-start mile which he set at Redcar at 91 mph.

He entered Gunga for the Eppynt road races in Wales in 1948 and in the big race of the day he was commandingly in front by half a lap. He raced over the hill to the finishing straight on full bore when the spectators began crossing the track. As a small girl slipped and fell off the banking into the road, George swerved to avoid her, ran up the bank into a field and as the front wheel on Gunga settled deep into a ditch, George was flung off and hit the ground, his face buried in a pile of stones. He was rushed to Gloucester Hospital some 90 miles away, badly hurt. They did a good skin grafting job on his face, though the scars were always visible. He was moved to Hill End Hospital at St. Albans and as he recovered he used to visit Mr Vincent and Mr Irving at the works. *I'd like you to enter Gunga so that I can ride at the next Dunholme meeting,* said George to Mr Irving one weekend. *I want to prove I haven't lost my nerve after the accident.* Mr Vincent agreed. There was strong opposition with Harold Daniel and Artie Bell on Nortons and the formidable AJS team of Bill Doran, Ted Frend and Jock West. Because Gunga was a 1000 cc machine George had to be content to start from the back row, but he made good progress even to the first corner and ended the race splitting the Nortons and AJSs and finishing an impressive third. When

The first time the racing Grey Flash appeared in public was at Eppynt. After going well, George crashed, leaving a good percentage of his face on the road.

at the end of the race George was only too anxious to tell me that the machine didn't handle as well with some new forks I had fitted as with the original ones, I knew he hadn't lost his nerve. He never even mentioned it, nor did I, and George continued to race and test ride with all his old flourish and courage.

The author on the experimental 'test house' Vincent Rapide in 1948.

George and his wife, Ada, with Mr and Mrs Brown senior and Norman Brewster and his wife, at Cadwell Park in the 1940s. The machine is a Series A Replica.

All set for the 1948 Clubman's TT. It was to be a hectic experience for the race-mad George. *(S. R. Keig)*

For all its modest beginnings, Gunga Din turned out to be a magnificently successful machine in the safe and capable hands of George. I would say that 1949 was the most impressive season, with George taking Gunga to a whole series of successes in a wide variety of events: in 1000 cc races at Ansty and Haddenham, an invitation race at Blandford; numerous sprints, including an impressive display along the front at Hartlepool in a race for unlimited class machines, and hill climbs such as Shelsley Walsh. George and Gunga were supreme in them all and it was George and the faithful Gunga who won again in a ten-lap scratch event for solo machines from 491 cc – 1000 cc in the first post-war meeting to be held at Silverstone.

In fact, there was no-one more successful than George at Shelsley Walsh. He competed there for the first time in 1948 and in a devastating run of 37.13 seconds broke the course record, for both bikes and cars. It was just the beginning for he went back annually for sixteen years and won handsomely every year, picking up the £30 prize money almost as a matter of routine. Big names like Noel Pope, Freddie Frith, Les Graham and many others, on a variety of impressive-sounding machines, did all they could to beat him, but without success.

Racing through Parliament Square in the 1948 TT. *(Motor Cycle Weekly)*

George continued to race Gunga Din until he left Vincents in 1951. It was used largely by Vincents as a mobile test bed and was not substantially different from the factory's production models, the factory's Black Lightning racer owing a lot to it. It had a 'cleaner' outward appearance than the pre-war Series A Rapide, the only oil pipes showing being the feed and return to the tank.

Brief specification of Gunga Din as George raced the machine in 1951 was:

Engine: 50° V-twin 1000 cc ohv; valve operation by high camshafts and short push-rods.
Ignition: magneto.
Transmission: primary drive via triple-row chain with slipper tensioner to four-speed gearbox in unit with engine; final drive by chain.
Frame: box-girder backbone, incorporating steering head and oil tank, bolted to cylinder heads; rear suspension by triangulated swinging fork with springs anchored to rear of box girder.
Forks: Girdraulic girders.

The great push home after running out of fuel on the Mountain in the Clubman's TT of 1948.

Finishing ... after the great push home. *(Motor Cycle Weekly)*

The drama ends as (above) George is helped in after finishing and establishing a record lap *(Salmond Photography)*, and (below) with a welcome drink at journey's end. *(Motor Cycle Weekly)*

There was no doubt that Gunga was a heavy machine. But in the famous article in *Motor Cycling* of November 13, 1947, in which Charles Markham was responsible for christening Gunga, he reported: *In spite of its size, Gunga Din conveys an indefinable feeling of safety at high speed, difficult to express but usually described in the hackneyed phrase 'race breeding'.*

Remember Honda's revolutionary slogan of many years later which got the fans excited: *race bred!* So what's new?

Charles' and Phil's article followed the former's request to Phil Irving to borrow George's very quick 'slightly tuned' standard Series B Rapide for a weekend of really rough testing. And the famous machine acquired its equally famous name following Markham's original introduction to his article. He quoted Kipling's famous lines:

> "Though I've belted you and flayed you
> By the livin' Gawd that made you
> You're a better man than I am Gunga Din."

It was also about 1948, I think, that Mr Vincent decided to turn the Number 49 shed into a special assembly department and as I was too busy with development work to build special engines, Dennis Minett was put in charge, with Stan Duddington and Jack Lazenby also very much involved. George used to test all the special bikes at Gransden airfield. In the winter it could be bitterly cold there and I remember we used to take with us a five gallon oil drum pierced with holes and a supply of coke to keep us warm. We would call at a little shop in Gransden and buy bread, butter and a tin of beans. George used to get on with his testing while I prepared beans on toast and when the food was ready I would wave him in. The sophistication of it all!

One test ride I still remember vividly was the Black Lightning which American Rollie Free ordered in an effort to break the American National Record, then standing at 136 mph. I built the engine in the test house — polished conrods and flywheels, cylinder heads opened out from 1 1/8 to 1 3/16 inch with 1 3/16 inch carbs, mark 2 cams, compression ratio 12.75 with 7/22 racing pistons, an exhaust pipe 1 5/8 by 56 inches long, and intermediate gears in the gearbox. On the test bed the drive side mainshaft broke when the engine was on full power, so off came the engine with George helping, and I had to strip it down, assemble new flywheels, fit them into the engine and re-time the valves and magneto.

It was one helluva rush because the bike was due for dispatch the very next day, so once we'd obtained a few readings on the brake test, Mr Irving

At Brough, Yorkshire, in 1949 Gunga Din is restrained by trainer George Brown. *(Geroge Schofield)*
Stopping at the pits to refuel during the 1949 Clubman's TT. *(Salmond Photography)*

George showing his paces at Shelsley Walsh where he was to become virtually unbeatable. The year is 1949. *(Guy Griffiths)*

Another win for Gunga Din at Silverstone; in 1949. *(Motor Cycle Weekly)*

The maestro takes Gunga Din to a record win at Goodwood in 1951. *(Motor Cycle Weekly)*

suggested that George and I take the bike to Gransden. George did a few runs down the straight at 145 mph. Mr Irving seemed well satisfied and called it a day. Just as well, for a few more runs at that speed could have spelt disaster, we later discovered, because when we examined the bike we found that the bolt fastening the rear mudguard had been fitted upside down. At speed the tyre had flung itself 1½ inches up and the bolt had cut a deep ridge into the tyre, dangerously close to the tube. A tyre failure at that speed could have been very nasty.

The bike was finally tested, crated and shipped to America the next day as scheduled and Rollie Free smashed the National record on Bonneville Salt Flats, Utah, first with a speed of 148.00 mph and later with a speed of 150.85 mph — with the bike virtually straight out of the crate.

George also did all the test riding when Mr Vincent decided he would develop a Comet for racing, and he did quite a bit of work on the frame, drilling and generally lightening. I remember George really did thrash the bike when we again went up to Gransden, this time with Mr Vincent. Up the runway, it was 80 mph in first, 100 in second, up to 110 mph in third and 115 mph in fourth at 8000 revs and on pool petrol. At first George and I called it the Eppynt Comet, since its first meeting was at Eppynt in Wales. Then Mr Vincent, since we already had the Lightning Twin, said we ought to call it the Grey Flash . . . and another historic Vincent was born.

George and I were also very much involved with the only Vindian that was ever made — a unique hybrid comprising an American Indian motor cycle frame and the Vincent twin-cylinder Rapide engine. The crates containing two Indian machines arrived at Stevenage from America only a week before the 1949 TT Races and as Vincents were entered in the Clubmans races — and I was preparing the two machines entered to Black Lightning specification — there was very little time to work on this new project. Phil Irving and welder Bill Munsden helped George and myself and we managed to get the work done before the TTs. When finished the Vindian, as it was known, handled like a dream. You could literally ride a circle with just one hand on the handlebars without fear of falling off. Mr Irving, George and I used to take it in turns to ride it to and from work and it would go up to 115 mph with no strain.

At the time I believe the Indian company were interested in marketing their machine powered by the Vincent engine, but nothing came of the project because, as I was later told, the Indian people became too impressed with the standard Vincent machines and thought they could sell them in America. Anyway, we were later told to take the engine from the frame, refit the Indian engine, re-crate the bike and dispatch both crates back to America. The crate containing the second bike was never opened. Sad, because the idea seemed sound and the bike certainly had possibilities.

Chapter 5

Racing on the Isle of Man

VINCENT BEGAN to move away from motor cycle manufacture in 1953 when they started to concentrate on the development of the Picador target aircraft engine. This was seen as an important government project, since the Picador engine was to be used to power a radio-controlled pilotless target aircraft. The government and the Ministry of Supply had insisted that the engine for the aircraft be British. There was no small British aero engine available and although several manufacturers were approached, none was interested. Mr Vincent, however, would accept any challenge and he jumped at it. The new unit began life as a Black Shadow engine and I was very much involved with the project, which was for me, personally, an invigorating experience.

The engine was to be fuel injected to eliminate any possibility of fuel starvation when the aircraft was in flight and, above all, when it was blasted into the air by rockets. I drew a Black Shadow engine from the engine assembly line with standard heads and 1 1/8 inch carbs. I dismantled the engine to check that everything was in order and then did a complete re-assembly job to fit in with the specifications and the objectives stated.

When it was complete we found that there was so much power going through the main shafts that the drive side used to move in the flywheel, so they were welded in. After numerous adjustments the engine performed well on the test bed so that by the autumn of 1952 everything was ready for aircraft flying trials at the end of the year, and which were scheduled to take place in the Libyan desert. At one point I thought I might be in attendance, but Mr Vincent would have none of that and said I was much more valuable at Stevenage. At my suggestion, Jack Lazenby went in my place and spent a happy, interesting, if busy time in the Libyan desert, returning bronzed and fit to the works during the second week in May.

Further trials were held that year at Monorbia and Castle Martin in Pembrokeshire, with Jack again in attendance. Further modifications were made and Jack and I went to De Havillands when the engine was fitted with thermal couplings to test it for air flow round the cylinder heads and barrels. In fact it was after the engines had been returned to Stevenage for further work on them that we required additional labour at Vincents, to cope with the work, and two men and an apprentice were taken on. Terry Wade and Bill Mason were the time-served engineers and, would you believe, a young and inexperienced apprentice called John Surtees was the third person.

Unfortunately, George had less to do as the business swung away from motor cycles. Moreover, the Vincent factory had sadly seen its most harmonious days. George was the first to leave, to be followed by chief engineer Alec Mitchell, who left at the end of 1952 to join Rolls-Royce at Crewe. Alec's position was taken by C.F. Braun, who turned out to be a good chief engineer. Jack Williams, who was development engineer on the Picador, left at the end of 1953 to become racing manager and development engineer at AJS. Major Honeychurch took over from Jack and was known as Technical Liaison Officer, dealing mainly with government contracts. Braun then left the company, to be followed shortly after by George Buck, who went to Vauxhall Motors and, later, Jaguar. It was all rather hectic and unsettling. Jack Williams tried to persuade me and Jack Lazenby, who worked on Special engines, to go with him to AJS. But Jack and I didn't fancy the upheaval of moving house and decided to stay with the Stevenage concern. Another departure around this time was John Surtees. John, even as an apprentice at the Vincent factory, had ambitions to be a professional road racer. Early experience in grass track racing led to success on a 500 cc Vincent Grey Flash and then recognition as a private entrant on a 500 cc Manx Norton. When George turned down an offer to join Norton, the famous team signed John, and he was on his way to a fabulous career.

You didn't have to be far sighted to see the way the wind was blowing with Vincents. By 1952 the firm was struggling and in 1954 gave up altogether.

George had, for some time, thought about setting up in business. He was by 1951 perhaps one of the most prolific all-round racers in the country, competing regularly and with a good deal of success in sprints, hill climbs and road races.

That year he decided to make the break and set up a motor cycle workshop business in Stevenage. It began in a small way on a capital of just £33; he used part of the local Ford dealership showroom in Stevenage as his base. He secured the agency for Francis Barnett, Norman and Velocette motor cycles and also accepted a number of special projects. One interesting

Chapter 5/59

Racing in the 1950s at Boreham Wood, with John Surtees (Vincent) leading George Brown (Norton).

assignment came from Air Vice Marshall 'Pathfinder' Bennett, who asked George to produce a Lightning engine suitable for his hill climbing racing car. I used to help George in my spare time and had enormous fun with this particular project. My job was to convert a standard Rapide into a full Lightning and the results were most satisfactory, since the Air Vice Marshall reportedly did very well with it at Shelsley Walsh, Prescott and in other important hill climbs.

When George left Vincents he had to surrender his trials bike so he wrote to Norman for one. Norman didn't manufacture a trials bike as such, so they sent him a 197 cc standard bike and said if he wanted to, they were quite happy for him to convert it to his own liking. We both got stuck in. We fitted a 21 inch front wheel, set the front forks up to give more ground clearance, and introduced an upswept pipe and aluminium guards back and front. George, with his usual enthusiasm, went off to challenge the world and did very well with it, winning quite a number of events. Norman were so pleased that they borrowed it back and used it as the prototype for a trials bike of their own, sending the original back to George as a present: though I'm sure they didn't cut him in on a royalty basis or give him a fee for using his ideas!

By this time Vincents had finished racing, but George was still as enthusiastic as ever. So we decided between us to make a Vincent racing twin of our own. We joked about it. *With what you know about engine building and me riding it, we've a good chance of producing a world beater,* said George, little realising at the time how near to reality his remarks would be. For the bike which emerged was Nero, certainly George's most famous bike of all. George went in search of and finally bought a burnt out Vincent Rapide from a garage in Mill Hill. He paid only £5 for it and I built the engine in my spare time with hand-made cams and high lift rockers. But I'm moving a little too far ahead. The birth, development and success of the famous Nero is dealt with in the next chapter, so for now let me concentrate on George's other activities at this time.

For someone who later became so famous in one very specialised branch of motor cycle sport, George was very much an all rounder at this point in his career and he was an extremely enthusiastic road racer. In fact, Nero was built originally as a general purpose bike. Before Nero, however, George bought a Manx Norton from Phil Heath and when he could find time from his business, he used to ride it at meetings.

Later the Norton gave way to a 350 cc AJS 7R Boy Racer, bought from Hallens of Cambridge, the machine Albert Moule had ridden in the 1951 TT, when he retired. After we had both worked hard on it, George raced it so well in tests at Gransden airfield that he decided to enter it in the 1952 Junior TT. That famous private tuner and entrant Joe Potts already had George entered on his 500 cc Norton and I was lucky to be given time off from Vincents to take care of George's bikes on the Island.

It reveals much about the way we went about things in those days when I say that the trailer on which we carried George's AJS was built out of a Jowett chassis!

It was a perfect morning, an hour before the start of the Junior TT of 1952. The *TT Special* reported: *The view across the island was crystal clear and the grey hills stood crisp against the sky. There was a light breeze blowing the clouds and sweeping the roads cool. The Glencrutchery Road was buzzing with activity, pit attendants laying out their stalls ready for the start and the riders bringing out their bikes from the marquee and giving them a final check. Everyone was at attention as the National Anthem sounded over the loudspeakers — a signal that the Lieutenant Governor of the Isle of Man had arrived. Then, at 9.15 am the siren blasts indicating that the riders can now take up their positions on the road and start warming up their engines. Four minutes to go and the riders are formed up behind the squad of Boy Scouts, who carry the flags of the represented nations. The timekeeper raises the Union Jack, brings it down again, and the race is on.*

Chapter 5/61

By 1951 – two famous machines and more and more trophies. *(Leonard Blakey)*

Geoffrey Duke, the previous year's winner, was away first, tucked in neatly behind the flyshield of his Norton. Then, at ten second intervals, the other riders followed. George was going well on the first lap — and we gave him a signal to let him know the good news — duelling with Arthur Wheeler on his Velocette for 12th place. Second time round George had overtaken Wheeler and was now up in 10th position. The AJS seemed to be going faster as George raced towards the Mountain for the fifth time . . . . now in seventh place. And we were thrilled to see him not only hold this position but improve it, finishing the race in sixth position behind winner Geoff Duke, Reg Armstrong, Rod Coleman, Bill Lomas and Syd Lawton. It was a magnificent effort on George's part, for this was his very first major race as a private entrant and only his second appearance in the TT. George's lap times were as follows: (1) 27m 10s, (2) 26m 35s, (3) 26m 30s, (4) 27m 20s, (5) 26m 35s, (6) 26m 34s, (7) 26m 51.4s. His total time was 3 hours, 7 mins, 33.4 secs., to give an average speed of 84.50 mph. This compared with 90.29 mph of the winner Geoff Duke, but was less than two minutes slower than Bill Lomas, placed fourth.

Riding a 7R AJS in the Junior TT of 1951.

We all attended the prizegiving at the Villa Marina in Douglas that evening, but then it was back to work again preparing for Friday's Senior race. Weather conditions were again ideal in the morning, not much sun but good visibility. Punctual to the second, the siren screamed the ten o'clock warning and after Geoff Duke again lead the field away, all the remaining riders moved off at 10 second intervals with no problems. We focussed on George's progress and found him lying tenth on the first lap, with the bike running sweetly. After beating off a challenge from Tom McEwan the second time round, George had moved up to eighth position by lap 3. Duke was leading from Les Graham, riding the four cylinder MV Agusta. On the fourth lap Bill Lomas flashed past the start line on the AJS Porcupine. Off the leaderboard there was a stern fight for seventh place, Rod Coleman on an AJS beating off a hectic challenge from the Nortons of Syd Barnett and George.

He slipped to eighth again on the fourth lap, but at the start of the fifth Geoff Duke grabbed our attention as he raced into the pits and overshot, his pit attendant alongside him in a flash. The clutch on his Norton had locked solid, so Geoff disgustedly eased off his helmet and called it a day. Les Graham on the powerhouse MV was now in the lead and George, battling on, was still eighth behind Bill Lomas.

On the sixth lap Reg Armstrong had gained 16 seconds as he rushed his Norton through Parliament Square and with 1½ laps still to go, Graham's lead was now down to only four seconds on corrected times. Armstrong seemed to be moving very quickly and had reduced the gap so that at the Bungalow he was level with Les.

But what had happened to George? He was still going magnificently and while the road racing giants with their special works machinery battled it out for the top placings, George's aim was to keep the Norton going sweetly and to make sure of finishing. As Les Graham's MV Agusta leaked oil, saturating the bike and gear lever, making gear changes difficult and also bending some of the valves, Armstrong increased his lead and ended the day with a Senior TT victory, with Les Graham second. George kept going and finished in seventh position — a very creditable performance. So in the Isle of Man in 1952 George was able to attend the TT winners' ceremonies at the Villa Marina to collect two well-earned replicas. And George said he reckoned no other private entrant had that year done better. In fact at the Senior prizegiving, George's son Antony caused a minor sensation. This is how the *Isle of Man Weekly Times* reported the incident: *Forty men and one little boy received awards from the hands of His Excellency the Lieutenant Governor (Sir Geoffrey Bromet) at the Senior TT Race prize distribution in the Villa Marina on Friday evening, witnessed by some 8,000 people. For the little boy, 5-years-old Antony Brown, son of TT rider George Brown, of Stevenage, Herts., it was one of the most momentous moments of his life.*

When his father made his way through the crowd to receive his replica, Antony ran after him, but hesitated as his father mounted the platform. But the Governor beckoned him to come up and handed him the prize.

Whether riders and their mechanics today have the same fun on the Isle of Man I just don't know, but in the 1950s there was always a great deal of skylarking among the riders and often, it has to be said, there was little concession to restraint or gentlemanly conduct. I remember George and I on one occasion putting strips of paper between the points of Dickie Dale's MG sports car and with great amusement watching him trying to start it as we lurked in the shadows of the hotel doorway.

Another time we put holly leaves and a scrubbing brush in his bed and you could hear him all over the hotel, if not across the length and breadth of the Island, when it was time for him to turn in. But Dickie wasn't going to accept that without retaliation. The next morning we were walking past his bedroom window when George and I were suddenly saturated. We looked up to see Dickie Dale, engulfed in laughter, holding an empty chamber pot. Ugh! But all the joking and pranks were taken in good part and there was always a wonderful feeling of comradeship along with the highly competitive atmosphere.

George's business was doing well so he decided it was time to make the next move. He took over a shop opposite the Vincent Number 1 factory and I helped him to move all the equipment one weekend so that he could carry on doing repairs in the workshop at the rear until we reconditioned and painted the inside and outside of the new building. To celebrate the opening George arranged a presentation of road racing films at the old town hall in Stevenage. It was a big attraction and a huge success. He took over the agency for Vincent and sold quite a number of Black Princes and Black Knights. His order through Vincent of the NSU, which by this time Vincent were distributing in Britain on a short term arrangement with the German factory, quickly reached about 30 a week — no mean order for those days — and he had the very last Black Knight to come out of the factory, for a customer in London.

George was keen to go to the TT again the following year (1953) and Mr Vincent once again gave me permission to accompany him to look after the bikes. After the 1952 TT George had sold his AJS Boy Racer to Maurice Brierley, who also ran a Vincent Rapide which he later used in sprints, with sidecar attachment. Joe Potts had again entered George in the Senior on his short stroke Norton and for the Junior event, in place of the earlier AJS, George bought a brand new 350 cc AJS racer. As the year before, I rode the AJS down to the start for George to begin practice and he rode the Norton. That first morning the AJS proved troublesome. The release valve in the flywheels stuck and oil gushed out of the drive side mainshaft, covering

George and myself. I had to take the bike to the AJS workshops in Douglas to have new flywheels fitted. With practice week over, George and I got down to checking and wire-locking all nuts and bolts and anything else which might conceivably become loose. George again rode exceptionally well, finishing 8th by our calculations. But then the official results were announced and George was put down as finishing 16th. We simply couldn't believe it and George went mad.

It appeared that the A-CU official timekeeper had mis-read his stop-watch and inadvertently placed George in the lower position. Although George did a lot of protesting, the results, as given, had to stand since the officials had given placings to all the other riders, but George was given his silver replica. It was bitterly disappointing and a most unsatisfactory outcome and the presentation of the replica didn't really compensate George for the injustice.

George negotiates Windy Corner in the Junior TT of 1952. He finished sixth.

Although we were unaware of the tragedy and drama that was to follow in the Senior event that year, George was still bristling about the mix-up in the Junior event as we prepared for the Senior race. At this stage in his career, George was still very interested in hill climb events and displaying a remarkable aptitude for sprinting as well as road racing. Little did we know that the very next race was destined to change the course of that career dramatically and that George would turn his back on road racing for ever from that point on.

It was the 35th Senior TT. There were 88 entries. Patches of mist shrouded the Mountain in the morning, to clear later in the day, but by then the career of the great Les Graham was almost at an end.

Les was well liked and much respected as a man as well as a motor cycle racer and George and he knew each other well. Just before the start Les bet George — who was drawn to be flagged away earlier than Les — that he would pass him *before* Bray Hill on the first lap. But he didn't — for George was already on his way down Bray Hill when Les thundered up on the MV Agusta. George won the bet, but he was destined never to collect his winnings. He was having a good race and the Norton sounded as sweet as a nut, not even the suggestion of a miss from the engine. After Les had passed him and gone ahead, an eye witness said Les's MV Agusta was rocketing down Bray Hill at a speed never seen on the Isle of Man before and he seemed to be struggling to maintain control. Les was in second position, but after leaving the dip of Bray Hill a full lock wobble developed and just over the rise on the way to Quarter Bridge, a cloud of dust and a pall of black smoke were ominous signs of the tragedy. George was not far behind Les when the accident happened and was unable to take avoiding action. At a speed said to be approaching 140 mph he had no option but to race headlong into the dense smoke pall and straight into the wreckage of Les's crashed MV Agusta. The impact was appalling. The petrol tank of the MV exploded, George was showered with burning petrol and with his clothing ablaze, was flung 300 yards. After somersaulting, bouncing and rolling, he finished up ten feet in the air, caught in the branches of a small tree. Shocked and dazed, he immediately and instinctively unhooked himself and staggered back onto the road . . . to be very nearly hit by Geoff Duke as he roared past the wreckage which now littered the road.

Les had died instantly when he crashed, but George had been saved by a miracle. He was badly shaken, but had escaped serious injury. Although Les's death and his own miraculous escape were to affect his future racing, he didn't immediately condemn the TT. He told a reporter shortly after the disaster: *I agree that the races are getting very gruelling and that the speeds of today's powerful machines are becoming too great for the Island's course,*

Chapter 5/67

Record-breaking at Brighton in the 1950s. *(James Prymer)*

but I don't agree that racing should end there. You mustn't halt progress. If you stop the TT Races you can halt lots of other things, including jet flying. Our aim is to improve the strain of motor cycles, to breed better machines and make them safer for the general public to ride.

When the accident happened I lost all interest in the race and dashed back from Ramsey, where I had my machine, to race as fast as I could along the coast road to Douglas, where George was already at the hotel recovering. His £450 worth of Norton was a complete write-off and I couldn't believe the insensitivity of some people as I saw them taking bits off and carting them away as souvenirs.

It didn't really occur to me that we wouldn't be on the Isle of Man for the TT Races the following year, but long before that George had decided to give up road racing, largely because of what had happened to Les.

Chapter 6

Nero and Record Breaking

FOR SOME 15 years the Vincent-powered Nero was to be George's life. Through that highly-dependable, ultra-fast machine he became internationally famous, a hero among the growing numbers of sprint enthusiasts. Yet the start of all was modest and casual in the extreme. Les's fatal crash had completed George's disenchantment with road racing, which was rapidly becoming financially prohibitive at top level for all, except the few with works contracts. At the same time sprinting was capturing renewed attention so George considered that here was a chance to make his mark by doing what dad had done in the 1920s. Moreover his success with Gunga Din made him determined to continue in some form of motor cycle sport.

George's first priority was to find an old Vincent Rapide and luckily he heard from an insurance company about a burnt-out wreck which he found discarded in a corner of a garage in Mill Hill, North London. The previous owner had apparently lost control of the bike which alarmingly was said to have ended up on the top of a single decker bus somewhere near Staples Corner! George went to see it and bought it as scrap for £5. We built up the bike as a Black Lightning, using bits and pieces from Gunga Din, which George felt by this time had served its purpose. A phenomenal amount of work was required but as Nero began to take shape George got more and more excited with its potential.

Although Nero was Vincent-powered, it was always a totally private venture financed by George alone and therefore the factory had no control over our activities. George wasn't even employed by Vincent at this time and I was soon to leave to go full time into George's motor cycle business, so we had a completely free hand concerning modifications. Over the years Nero was changed considerably to meet the increasing demands of record breaking. George replaced the crankshaft with one of his own design and increased the compression ratio to 13:1. It was stripped and rebuilt numerous times, but time and again Nero excelled. In 1953 alone, in only eight months of competition, George rode Nero to five Fastest Times of the Day at places like Shelsley Walsh, Abridge, Pendine sands and Brighton.

It was in October that year that George took Nero to Pendine sands for a special occasion. Vic Willoughby, that highly respected technical authority on motor cycles and now retired as technical editor of *Motor Cycle Weekly*, had during the TT fortnight in June accepted an invitation from George to have a gallop on Nero. That's how the pair of them, together with Nero, came to be at Pendine one weekend and on the Sunday had a happy time putting Nero through its paces. Though there was nothing official about the occasion, both George and Vic were serious enough about putting Nero to the test and if the timing arrangements were a little extraordinary, they were every bit legitimate. They consisted of two radio cars, one at each end of a measured half mile. These facilities were provided by a couple of motor cycle enthusiasts from the Ministry of Supply's Experimental Establishment at Pendine, Major Bahin and Signalman Omand, who produced an accurate timing system. This was highly desirable because piloting Nero on a sand surface, with the machine's high power-to-weight ratio, wheelspin would have made converted rev-meter readings inaccurate.

Sand, sand and more sand. Pendine Beach in 1961 during record attempts. *(Motor Cycle Weekly)*

Chapter 6/71

Nero at Pendine. Note the no-tread tyres. *(Motor Cycle Weekly)*

Vic Willoughby riding Nero at Pendine. *(Motor Cycle Weekly)*

The objective was that both George and Vic should take Nero to a speed in excess of 150 mph — not exceptionally fast perhaps, but there was still something arbitrarily magical about the 'ton and a half' target. Even before the weekend Vic had regarded Nero in a class of its own among standing-start sprint two-wheelers and his Pendine experience did nothing to soften that opinion.

Both George and Vic found that over-exuberant use of the twist grip when accelerating could provoke wheelspin in all four gears, but when handled correctly Nero's rock-steady steering at high speed was extremely impressive. I remember both George and Vic agreeing that, to quote Vic's subsequent article in *The Motor Cycle, 'there was something fundamentally satisfying about the type of power which, to the accompaniment of the slightly uneven lilt of the V-twin's exhausts, sends the rpm indicator rocketing round the dial, irrespective of which gear is engaged!'* Vic said that the combination of rock-steady steering, a high top gear ratio, and the broad expanse of the open beach, tended to minimise the impression of speed and added, to which George smilingly agreed: *That is, until you glance at the 'moving' sand beneath the bike wheels . . . and then the effect is alarming.*

Early in 1954 George and I began the first of Nero's numerous conversions. George Buck, technical adviser at Vincent, arrived at work one morning and said he was giving in his notice to Mr Vincent, as he had secured a job at Jaguar's car factory in their experimental department. Before he left he kindly did some drawings which enabled George and me to replace the normal Vincent cantilever swinging arm with our own special swinging arm. This, we calculated, would improve road holding generally and give greater stability on corners. It involved cutting the Vincent ones off the casting and brazing on Velocette swinging arm legs. We also fitted AJS Porcupine front forks and a 19 inch front wheel. The telescopic front forks George got from Jock West, who was sales director at AJS and who had been trying to get Vincent to use them. He got George to try them out as a kind of test.

George's retail business was flourishing and Vincent's was obviously ailing. When Stan Duddington, who was a mechanic with George, decided to leave for a job in Hemel Hempstead, George asked me if I would go and help him in his business full time. So it was on October 29, 1954, that I left the Vincent factory. George and Nero were getting better at sprinting all the time and with the Vincent frame, 19 inch front wheel and high bottom gear, set new records at meeting after meeting, including Sherburn aerodrome in Yorkshire, Shelsley Walsh, Brighton and Prescott. In fact George and Nero were such a successful combination that it was then that we decided to concentrate on trying to make Nero into the perfect bike for breaking world and race meeting records. On the small lathe which George had bought, I got down to turning the necessary parts needed to fit the

Nero in road racing form. *(Motor Cycle Weekly)*

A close up of Nero, showing the sidecar attachment arrangement. *(J. H. Cuff)*

AJS forks onto the Vincent backbone. Velocette rear fork legs were welded to the Vincent bearing housing, which held the Timkin taper bearings. We used the base of the flywheel centre to set up the housing and fork legs with a Vincent rear wheel spindle for the right distance for the wheel. We also fitted Velocette rear dampers. When the bike was finished, the wheelbase was as for the featherbed Norton — 52 inches long — to improve the handling capabilities. We then took the bike to Gransden Airfield for George to ride and check the handling. After racing round the track he said it steered and handled like a dream.

While the short frame for Nero had been suitable for road racing and hill climbs, it was too short for sprints. George couldn't prevent the front wheel from lifting on acceleration and he therefore lost valuable time. We decided to bring the engine nearer to the front wheel by lengthening the rear swinging arm by 3 inches and lowering the engine to within 2 inches from the ground. This corrected the wheel lifting and subtracted a good two seconds from Nero's time.

Later George had enquiries to build three basic road versions of Nero — one for a doctor in Scotland, another for a Frenchman, and a third for an Eastbourne shop-keeper. It took quite a time, as I had other work to do, and George had to look after the shop, but we finished them after working long hours at night. George charged £450 for them (ridiculously cheap even by 1956 standards — it was largely a labour of love for George). The doctor in Scotland wanted his for ordinary running and for use as a sprinter, the shop-keeper had his in road trim and used it purely as a domestic machine, while the Frenchman used to go hill climbing on his. Two of them at least were still in use more than 20 years later. George had many more people wanting him to make similar machines for them, but we just didn't have the time.

George had sprint wins and seconds at Banbury, Ramsgate, Chester, Long Marston, Bristol's Goram Fair, Shelsley, Brighton, Pontypool and Jersey. He and I went with Arthur Breeze and Jack Terry to Jersey. Arthur (500 cc) and Jack (350 cc) won their classes all right, but Nero, with full fairing, had a narrow escape on its last run. The race meeting officials did not anticipate that George would be going as fast as he was at the end of the quarter mile run and had moved the crowd barrier forward. George hit it at 100 mph and both he and Nero ended up underneath a car. George was rushed to hospital with a suspected fractured collar bone and concussion. When I went to pick up the bike the fairing had three massive dents in the front of the nose, but there was no real damage to the bike. George had recorded the Fastest Time of the Day and won the States of Jersey Cup. I drove his car from Southampton to Stevenage with the bike on the trailer, as George had to stay in Jersey Hospital for a week. At the end of the week, the Jersey Club paid to fly George home with a nurse. I went to Heathrow to meet the plane and drive George home to Stevenage. When we checked Nero for alignment we were astonished to find no serious damage. The only thing we had to do was to send the fairing to the tinsmith to have the dents knocked out.

By 1959 Nero had long since become one of the most famous machines in British motor cycle sport. Compression ratio at that time was 25:1. Maximum rpm were some 6,800 and at this speed it produced about 85 bhp. George was always keen to improve the machine further and almost to the end of its record breaking days he and I worked on it regularly. However, once George had contemplated the idea of a supercharged counterpart, which eventually emerged as Super Nero, much of our time was diverted to the new machine.

Brief specification of Nero around 1959 was:

Engine: V-twin, 1000 cc ohv; valve operation by high camshafts and short push-rods.
Ignition: magneto.
Transmission: primary drive via triple-row chain with slipper tensioner to four-speed gearbox in unit with engine; final drive by chain.
Frame: box-girder backbone, incorporating steering head and oil tank, bolted to cylinder heads; rear suspension by swinging fork.
Forks: AMC telescopics.

George and Cliff's father — their sporting inspiration — with an Austin 7, heavily inscribed for a local carnival, in 1955.

George soon recovered from his Jersey crash and in 1960 we made more modifications to Nero. New carb inductions were made up for the 1 7/32 inch GP carbs and we lowered the rear end by fitting shorter rear damper springs. The first meeting with these modifications was at Blackpool and George made Fastest Time of the Day. After strengthening the bottom end we had no further trouble with main bearings and the big end. For the next meeting, at Chester, we fitted a modified Norton clutch with seven friction plates which we grafted to the Vincent clutch carrier to give us something more than the usual five-plated clutch. This was necessary to give Nero more grip on getaway. More over, the Vincent as standard had a centrifugal clutch so if the engine had seized it would have locked and there was nothing that could have been done to free it. This proved very successful at the meeting and also at the Radley Hill hill climb. George was getting so much power now from Nero — around 85 - 90 bhp — that the front wheel was again lifting in the air, so we decided to extend the rear end another 2½ inches. I also found that we would have to open the needle jets from 125 to 140 and the main jets from 1,700 to 2,000 for nitromethane.

It was about this time that George approached Tom Joy, technical manager of Avon, the tyre people, and asked him if he could make him something superior to the buffed and cross cut standard Safety Mileage covers that George used to have to grapple with because of Nero's power, with a view to greater things to come. This turned out to be a major move and, curiously, the initiative came from George himself. His shop in Stevenage often attracted visiting Americans, particularly around TT time, and it was from one such American visitor that George learned about a retread flat tyre called a slick which was being used in the United States. George told Avon and through Avon's agent in America, Tom Joy managed to get hold of one and tested it on the Avon rollers.

George also told Tom that the first 60 yards would always be crucial in sprinting so Tom lost no time in trying to come up with a compromise, bearing in mind what George had said. He got his specialists at Avon experimenting with many different compounds and rubbers trying to get near to the American sample. He came up with a cover to fit Nero's extra-wide 3 inch rim with a smooth flat tread as wide as would go between the rear forks. The tread was twice the width of a standard tyre — sensational for those days. George, Tom and I, with an Avon tyre fitter, went down to Gransden airfield to see George put it through its start paces. The results were good, so the next thing was to use it for sprints. George found that the wheelspin, though reduced, was not completely eliminated, but he had certainly proved the value of the new tyre for sprinters. These slick tyres were later tested at Brighton, Ramsgate, Chester, Witchford and Long Marston. George later rode my 250 cc NSU Max at Witchford in the standard class, which he won

Sliding round at the start with Nero during the Jubilee International Speed Trials at Brighton in 1955. *(Charles Dunn)*

Nero, with all-aluminium streamlining (inspired by BMW example) about to become airborne on Madeira Drive, Brighton, as George nears 190 mph in the National Speed Trials of 1958. *(Charles Dunn)* with an 18 second run — not at all bad in touring trim. At Long Marston George then broke the standing kilometre World record one-way run at 107 mph, with a misfiring magneto! It was then that George decided he would have a go at the kilometre World record on Nero at a later date. after the sidecar World record held by Florian Camathias on a BMW and Alfredo Milani's solo World record on a four-cylinder Gilera. That's really how George and myself, with Nero, and Pat Barrett, Bob Slater and Len Cole, all of them members of the National Sprint Association, and representatives from the Avon Tyre Company, found ourselves at Thurleigh Airfield on Saturday, October 29, 1960. We had scheduled this weekend as a serious preview for the record attempts, giving Nero a major testing and, above all, seeing how the Avon slicks would stand up to the strain. This is the weekend described in some detail in Chapter Two. Tom Joy of Avon's had claimed that the new slicks were okay up to 200 mph and we were happy to find during the weekend that his claims had not been at all extragavant. George considered it a marvellous tyre and it was therefore George's initiative which opened the way to the widespread use of slick tyres in motor cycle racing today.

But we're moving ahead too quickly.

Although George and Nero had claimed a good many successes in the early 1950s, we were still going through an experimental period, doing modifications on the machine and trying them out. In my opinion the modifications which contributed most importantly to Nero's performances as a sprint machine were new home-made camshafts with different lifts and closing rates, a much stronger flywheel assembly, locking the main bearings into the crankcase so they couldn't move (to prevent the engine from falling apart!), and the excellent basic design of the Vincent frame.

Shortly before Vincents closed down, George took over the agency for the Vincent Amanda water scooter, introduced in 1955. This was an interesting project which included an entirely automatic centrifugal clutch and self-recoil starter. It was a safe enough scooter if used in the right way, and in the event of a rider falling off or diving from the scooter, the throttle would close down to tick-over and the automatic clutch would disengage. Thus the craft would automatically stop moving. Sadly, it was ahead of its time, both in technical specification and in its appeal to the public. The emphasis on leisure pursuits which could have made it into a world beater had yet to come, and it never sold in satisfactory numbers.

Between 1955 and 1958 George's interest in sprinting and record breaking had developed rapidly and it was in 1958 that, through the initiative of George, Jack Terry, Len Cole and a few other riders, the National Sprint Association was formed. Road racing, by now increasingly the domain of works-sponsored teams, had become intolerably expensive for most private

Officially classified as the 998 cc Vincent Special, but known more affectionately as Nero. George at the Ramsgate Sprint Meeting in October 1959. (*J. H. Cuff*)

riders, some of whom were looking for a less expensive method of racing. George, for other reasons as we have seen, had already decided to move out of road racing, but the National Sprint Association was to give sprinters a much needed boost and a more official and authoritative voice and standing. Bemsee used to organise sprints at Ramsgate, but it was felt better to have a special organisation to concentrate on the interests of sprint riders.

A revamped Nero was taken to Shelsley Walsh and Leeds, but at the latter meeting the primary chain broke damaging the crankcase, engine and clutch sprockets. In 1958 George won nine times at sprints and hill climbs, including the Fastest Time of the Day for solo bikes along the promenade at St. Helier in Jersey, already described. It was coming back from this trip that George became more angry than I have ever seen him before. At Southampton the customs officials hardly touched our luggage, but insisted that we almost strip Nero threadbare. I suppose they felt we could be smuggling something into the country. We were already tightly scheduled for a sprint meeting at Brighton and George became more and more angry as the minutes ticked away in the customs sheds. He became so furious that the customs men had finally to bring in the police to calm him down. He was still bristling when we arrived at Brighton and in no mood to be done down by other competitors. He made Fastest Time of the Day without any problem!

It was in 1958 that George shattered the speed world by becoming the fastest man *in the world* to cover a kilometre from a standing start with any machine, four-wheeled or two. It happened at Brighton, the South Coast town in those days being the grand prix venue of the sprint world. To win at Brighton was a fantastic performance, because racing cars equipped with Spitfire aircraft engines under the bonnet used to compete there.

The Brighton speed trials in 1958 were the background to one of George's most outstanding triumphs. His previous best time for the distance had been 20.99 seconds, but on his record-breaking run he clipped more than a second and a half off that time to complete the run in 19.29 seconds. His average speed was 117 mph and his terminal speed exceeded 186 mph.

Speeds and figures can lose impact after a time so let's just put that performance in perspective. It says much for George's ability on Nero when you consider that only four other riders had ever covered the kilometre from a standing start at an average speed of 100 mph, whether on two wheels or four. For this distinction they received a special Silver Star from the National Sprint Association. The Association also had on offer a Gold Star counterpart as an acknowledgement for an average speed of 110 mph or more. George's performance not only won him the Silver and Gold awards, but his latest success earned him a second Gold Star and the instant recognition of the motoring as well as the motor cycle world.

George loved to surprise and confound his fans. The programme for the Brighton meeting had cast doubts on the possibility of George improving on his previous records. There was no malice in his joy, but he was delighted to prove them wrong and got almost as much pleasure from this as in actually reaching such a phenomenal speed.

Afterwards I dismantled Nero's engine for examination and found the drive side flywheel 0.015 inch and the timing side 0.005 inch out of true. This would have been acceptable for a standard bike, but certainly was not good enough for me . . . and Nero. So we decided to fit the new Picador flywheel set up, with the larger main bearing. First I turned the rim of the flywheels and then fitted 1 1/8 inch mainshafts with a double start oil pump worm. When I fitted the new main bearing in the crankcase I fitted plates to stop the bearings moving or coming out entirely, and this arrangement was maintained in Nero right through the machine's record breaking career. In fact, it is still on Nero to this day. With the standard Vincent, the flywheels had a habit of moving out of true and they used to wriggle the bearings out of the crankcase.

George didn't do too badly with Nero in 1959 and in 1960, of course, came his impressive runs, along with Maurice Brierley, at Thurleigh in pursuance of the Camathias and Milani World records. But 1961 was to prove a year of great impact and success.

Chapter 7

1961 and into the Big Time

OF ALL the wonderful times I shared with George I look back with perhaps the greatest nostalgia of all to 1961. Not that George was at his peak then as a sprinter. His greatest triumphs and most prolific times were yet to come. But the year brought more World records for George on Nero and mainly because of what lay ahead, I always look back on 1961 as the start of George's most exciting days.

The year started quietly enough with George and me preparing Nero for a test ride which Vic Willoughby wanted to make. Vic was always closely associated with George and the two of them were great friends. We used to see Vic on his visits to Vincent in the old days. Mind you, George got on well with most folk and made very few enemies indeed. We soon had everything ready and set off for Gransden airfield — Vic, George, myself, with Tim Hatton and Pat Barrett, who later was to work for me in George's workshop. Nero had been exhibited on the Avon stand at the recent Motor Cycle Show in London in sidecar trim so it was with the sidecar that Vic decided to make his first test. Then came a solo run. Both were perfect and really very impressive. Vic was no novice to the motor cycle business, but he was plainly astonished by Nero's power. In fact, Nero was pulling a 3.2 to 1 top gear, reaching 6,500 rpm (close on 170 mph) in a kilometre. Vic asked where all the power came from. George told him, smiling: *It comes from me and Cliff burning the midnight oil and working through the weekends.*

Following his experience Vic turned in an excellent article for *The Motor Cycle* (February 9, 1961) under the title 'Nero Away — But Fast'. His introduction was a fine piece of graphic writing and in my view encapsulated everything that George and Nero were about, in a mere 250 words. Vic wrote: *Whether you want the thrill of a lifetime or a first class fright, try this recipe. Take 3 cwt of motor cycle with 90 to 100 bhp under the tank and an Avon slick tyre at the back for real traction, clear the decks well ahead and squirt off the mark. More explicitly, get yourself a ride on George Brown's Nero and discover just how quickly the horizon can gather itself up and hurtle towards you.*

You know Nero, of course — the 998 cc Vincent-powered special on which George hoisted the world's sidecar sprint record to 98.98 mph last November before setting a new solo figure of 107.44 mph. But I'll wager those bare figures — average speeds for a kilometre from rest — convey little of George's and Nero's tremendous performance, except to those on the inside of sprinting. So for the benefit of those on the outside, let's get it in perspective.

Imagine George straddling Nero on the start line, bottom gear engaged, clutch and twistgrip at the ready. Visualise another rider, chin on tank, streaking up from the rear at a steady 107-plus. The instant our speedman flashes past, George drops the clutch and gives chase. A forlorn hope? Not a bit of it! Soon Nero is flat in second and the gap stops widening, then it is narrowing fast. By the time our speedman crosses the finish line, only 1094 yards away and well within sight of the start, George thunders past with some 60 mph to spare. That 20.82 seconds' drama is what it means to average 107.44 mph from rest.

We did a number of adjustments and modifications after the tests and in preparation for a National Sprint Association meeting at Snetterton, made a new swinging arm 6 inches longer than the previous one, with seat frame to match and 11 inch-long rear dampers. We modified the front forks by making the rebound springs longer; the inner rods we reduced by 1 inch. Once all this work was done George took Nero to have a full streamline fairing made in aluminium by a noted tinbasher at Ascot. He made a remarkable job of it. It was as smooth as silk and as polished as a jet fuselage. It was George's idea to add the streamlining. He had studied the example of Guzzi — with their scientific wind tunnel approach in Italy — and insisted on having streamlining for Nero. It was the first time that streamlining had been added to a sprint machine in Britain and, typical of George of course, he insisted on the best. Aluminium, for most people, would have been far too expensive. But where his riding and record breaking were concerned, George would always spend what he could and what he thought necessary to get the results. The new streamlining proved highly successful, probably adding as much as 10 mph to Nero's top speed. This encouraged George to enter what was the first ever sprint meeting to be held on the Isle of Man, with sprint bikes roaring along the Ramsey sea front. This enterprising move was the idea of the National Sprint Association and a lot of their members turned

George waits whilst Cliff changes plugs during the World record attempts at Thurleigh in 1960. *(Motor Cycle Weekly)*

out to ride. The event was organised by the Ramsey Motor Cycle Club. There was also a standard class for anyone on the Island with a standard bike who wished to try his luck. It's a pity that this latter idea didn't really catch the imagination and was later abandoned through lack of entries. George, who had been all for the idea, was disappointed that it didn't make more impact and was not repeated for standard machines. After a bit of bother with a misfiring magneto and a broken chain tensioner blade, George took Nero to a very satisfactory Fastest Time of the Day.

By now — midway through 1961 — George had won about a dozen sprint meetings during the year. A notable occasion was his Fastest Time of the Day — at 107 mph — at the Long Marston event. George's riding throughout the day was described by one observer as 'awe inspiring' and although ignition problems delayed his appearance on the start line for his first run, his take off left little doubt in anybody's mind that in 1961 Nero was the fastest accelerating motor cycle in the world. He could have taken the record on that occasion, but the timing gear failed to record properly, and he had to go through it all again. The new frame forks had improved Nero, the new fairing was highly successful, and Nero's starts were getting better and better. It was at this point that he decided particularly to have another go for Milani's solo World record. We fixed the dates, August 19/20, 1961, so we had plenty of time for preparation. George decided not to prejudice the attempts by doing a full programme of sprints in advance. In fact. he decided to pull out of all other sprint activity and the two of us concentrated fully on preparations for the record attempt. We made a completely new sidecar and to get the benefit of every possible bit of streamlining, used 1¼ inch x 5/8 inch oval tubing instead of the more customary strutted round tubing; and we made a new streamlined sidecar wheel. George also decided he would ride his 250 cc Ariel Arrow and because it was so fast, go for the 250 cc, 350 cc amd 500 cc solo records. The Ariel factory had supplied a bike and engine for us to work on. George made a trip to Ariel's factory with the engine to brake test it on their test bed with Val Page, the designer, while Pat Barrett, who was working for George by now, and I, set to work drilling and lightening the wheels and hubs of the Ariel. I also concentrated on preparing Nero. We organised things so that the third wheel we were preparing for Nero could also be fitted to the Ariel machine, so that should he wish, George could also make an attempt at the 250 cc sidecar record.

George took the new Nero fairing down to a specialist firm in London and had three fairings made in fibreglass from it. This was revolutionary at the time, but George reckoned the expense would be worthwhile since a fibreglass fairing was reputed to cut down the wind resistance quite considerably. We fitted one to the Ariel. As time drew near the tension mounted. Final adjustments were made. Loaded into George's brand new van were bikes, fuel, a mass of tools and spares . . . and by 5.00 am on Saturday, August 19, we were on our way. I remember thinking as we moved stealthily through the deserted streets of Stevenage that here we were on our way to make attempts on World records . . . and no-one knew about it.

At Thurleigh we went through similar formalities to our previous visit, giving our names and nationality, etc in turn. Under new regulations brought in that year, a record attempt could no longer be made if the wind was blowing at more than six knots. Wind was destined to play a significant part in our efforts that weekend. Soon after arriving at Thurleigh, George was ready to make the attempt with Nero but the A-CU and FIM officials, armed with the whirling anemometer, wouldn't let him run. It seemed like hours as we all waited . . . and waited for the wind to fall below the six knots mark. George was bright and cheerful and, undismayed, decided on a trial run with Nero, The bike behaved well and he returned to the start, re-set the gear change, and once again we all waited.

Within an hour the airfield was being lashed by heavy rain. Then our previous record attempts were given down-priority as the airfield was allocated to aircraft movement. All day we waited, becoming more nervous, disappointed and frustrated by the hour. Not until just after seven o'clock in the evening did the wind drop. Quickly George did two practice runs on Nero, but the compression on one cylinder had gone. I hastily took off the tappet covers and found one exhaust tappet had tightened. The pushrods were checked and adjusted and at precisely 7.55 pm George whipped Nero off the line. Two excellent runs gave him his best mean times ever, at 20.794 seconds, 107.81 mph. But as in the previous November, the figures were short of the required 1 per cent improved margin for the record. George made two more runs, but Nero started to misfire badly, I took the bike from him, loaded it into the van, and worked on it furiously. George was loathe to waste the time as the wind had now dropped, so while I worked like fury on Nero in the back of the van, George got rid of his tensions by belting the 250 cc Ariel up and down the runway ... and in so doing bettered three British standing kilometre records. It was a miracle. Two runs at a speed of 77.05 mph disposed of the 250 cc and 350 cc classes and even bettered the 500 cc figures, but the latter by less than the required one per cent for the record. George did another brace of runs immediately and put the issue beyond doubt, adding the 500 cc record with an impressive 77.5 mph.

As darkness closed in and racing stopped for the day, George rested and later slept, while Pat Barrett and I worked through the night and almost until dawn, stripping Nero, easing the rings on the front cylinder, and fitting a new piston on the rear cylinder as the ring grooves had broken away on the old piston. We also fitted a new magneto. Pat and I were red-eyed as George, up like the proverbial lark, emerged in fine spirits and almost before the anemometer could get into its stride, howled the Ariel through the speed traps at a mean speed of 106.69 mph. It was fast enough to take all the three British flying-start kilometre records (250 cc, 350 cc and 500 cc), but he holed a piston towards the end of the final return run. As I dismantled the Ariel and began fitting a new piston, George wheeled out Nero, but as he did so the wind got up again and the attempt was once more halted. Around mid-morning the wind dropped and George didn't waste time. Immediately he scorched off east with a getaway that was perfection, but he muffed a gear change. A desperate repeat run, with George changing gears almost continuously, gave him 20.64 seconds. On his return George was in stupendous form and we all cheered as his run was clocked at an unbelievable 20.505 seconds. His mean speed of 108.73 mph comfortably exceeded by the necessary one per cent Milani's World record. After almost a quarter of a century, the standing-start kilometre World record for 1000 cc solo machines, was back with Britain, thanks to George and Nero. It had been a life's ambition of George's to take this record and he had not only been successful in spite of the unfavourable weather conditions, but he had crucified it with

At Thurleigh, during the warming up period for an attack on the Italian Standing Start Kilometre Record when the fog lifts. Time: 3.45 am. Security looks on. *(Motor Cycle Weekly)*

his average of 108.73 mph. Milani's 1957 Gilera record had been conclusively bettered and George was a very happy man. Ironically, he had also settled the embarrassing outcome from the previous November, when his British record of 107.44 mph had been fractionally better than Milani's record, but the start-line infringement described in an earlier chapter had denied him the World record.

But our efforts weren't at an end yet. Immediately we hitched Nero to the sidecar and sent George off to beat his own sidecar record which he had set up the previous November. But an increasing wind unfortunately put paid to any more official attempts for the remainder of the day, though George, it should be recorded, did 105 mph unofficially in really quite difficult conditions. It was a physically and psychologically shattered small band of race-maniacs who arrived back in Stevenage, where the engines were stripped and measured by A-CU and FIM officials in the small hours of Monday morning.

Chapter 7/87

But the weekend had been a major success. George had captured the World's solo standing-start kilometre record with a time of 20.573 seconds and a speed of 108.73 mph on the 998 cc Vincent-powered Nero. With the 249 cc Ariel Arrow he had secured the British standing-start kilometre record in the 250 cc, 350 cc and 500 cc solo classes with a time of 28.863 seconds and a speed of 77.5 mph, and the British flying-start kilometre record, again in the 250 cc, 350 cc and 500 cc solo classes, with a time of 20.966 seconds and a speed of 106.69 mph. Not bad going when you consider that during the entire weekend there had been not more than a few hours of racing time available to us because of the weather conditions.

George had wanted also to go for the standing quarter and flying quarter records, but with these attempts denied to him because of the weather, he decided to return to Thurleigh the following month, September. We arrived with the same team early Saturday morning, but we very nearly had a disaster before we had even begun the record attempts. Pat Barrett rode Nero up and down the runway as a warm up for the world record-breaking machine and then I took the Ariel out for the same purpose. I was roaring down the centre of the runway at approaching 100 mph when out of the

Record breaking attempts at Thurleigh. The end of that line is 2¼ miles away and at 210 mph, it looks like a cotton thread. *(Motor Cycle Weekly)*

Waiting for the fog to lift at Thurleigh, but what about that shine! *(Motor Cycle Weekly)*

Super Nero being re-fuelled with 'liquid dynamite' at Thurleigh. *(Herts Pictorial)*

An inspiring combination. George Brown with his famous Nero outside George's Stevenage shop in 1961. (J. H. Cuff)

mist, coming onto me from the opposite direction, were two security Land Rovers, travelling in line abreast about 20 feet apart. I saw them just in time and could do nothing more than aim the Ariel directly between them. George was as white as a sheet when I arrived back at the airfield buildings. He had seen what had happened and felt sure there was no possible way that I could avoid an appalling crash. I'm not too sure whether it was me or the Ariel he was most concerned about!

George's aim was the standing quarter mile. This distance had only just been recognised for the purpose of British national records and George was determined to be the first man to hold the record. The following month would see the 1961 records day at Wellesbourne airfield in Buckinghamshire when other racers would almost certainly be going for the record. George again rode impressively, recording 10.489 seconds for the solo 1,000 cc class (a speed of 85.80 mph), and with the sidecar attached, 11.441 seconds (78.66 mph). They were formidable targets for future records and weren't in fact bettered until he himself improved them. When he took the Ariel out for the 250 cc flying quarter mile record he reached a remarkable time in one direction, flashing along at more than 130 mph. His average time for the two runs was 7.107 seconds, or 126.64 mph. Later in the day he established a new quarter mile standing-start record on the Ariel with a time of 14.323 seconds (62.84 mph).

Because of high winds George races a naked Nero along the front at Brighton in 1962.

George was really in scintillating form and later that same evening made a bid for the 1000 cc flying-start quarter mile record on Nero. He made one stupendous run, entering the timed stretch at 180 mph, but darkness was closing and the fog which had delayed the start in the morning returned. Sensibly, though George wanted the record, he only coasted over the fastest part of the distance. Even so he was timed at 150 mph!

It had been a hectic and tiring time for us all, but back in Stevenage Pat Barrett and I dismantled the bikes for examination and measuring by the FIM and AC-U officials. Then we set to work reassembling the bikes and finished about 4.00 am. Why? George, with Pat, was entered for competition at Tadcaster in Yorkshire the following day. I drove all the way up there, with George asleep for most of the journey. Pat took the honours in the sidecar class and George, bless him, swept the board and made Fastest Time of the Day. That was my boy!

Finishing the season in style, George travelled to Ramsgate and with the Ariel on the sea front quarter mile at the Sunbeam MCC meeting won the 250 cc class with 15.055, breaking the 1956 record of Jack Terry (Ariel) by one fiftieth of a second! On Nero he set Fastest Time of the Day with 11.805.

THURLEIGH, AUGUST 1961

His impressive World record apart, George secured seven British National records during the Thurleigh weekend in August 1961. Despite the weather it was generally acknowledged as a magnificent performance and certainly to my mind one of the highlights of George's career.

The complete dossier reads like this:

Standing-start kilometre, 1000 cc. Speed: 108.73 mph. Time: 20.573s. Machine: 998 cc Vincent Special (Nero) solo. Previous record by Alfredo Milani (Gilera) at 106.77 mph in 1957 at Monza, Italy.

Standing-start kilometre. Speed: 77.5 mph. Time: 28.863s. Machine: 249 cc Ariel Arrow. Classes: 250 cc, 350 cc and 500 cc solo. Previous records: 250 cc, J.S. Worters (Excelsior) 65.16 mph, 1926. 350 cc, G. Dance (Sunbeam) 71.69 mph, 1923. 500 cc, M.E. Davenport (HRD) 76,68 mph, 1927.

Flying-start kilometre. Speed: 106.69 mph. Time: 20.966s. Machine: 249 cc Ariel Arrow, Classes: 250 cc, 350 cc and 500 cc solo. Previous records: 250 cc, J.S. Worters (Excelsior) 88.99 mph, 1926. 350 cc, H. Le Vack (Coventry Eagle) 96.46 mph; 1925. 500 cc, H. Le Vack (New Hudson) 104.57 mph, 1927.

Note: George's 108.73 mph standing-start performance on Nero also bettered his own British 1000 cc solo record of 107.44 mph made in the previous November.

George was such a prolific and successful competitor that even exceptional rides are in danger of being overlooked. His memorable sprinting in 1961 shouldn't be allowed to obscure his hill climb achievements and at the annual meeting at Shelsley Walsh he completed the 1000 yard climb in 36.6 seconds, an average of 57 mph from a standing-start. It broke his own twelve year old record by just 0.53 of a second.

In 1961 ... Pat Barrett, brother Cliff Brown and George outside the Stevenage shop.

Chapter 8

The Birth of Super Nero

BY 1962 George had already accomplished more than would have been enough for most men. He had shown his prowess as a road racer and was acknowledged as one of the country's top hill climbers and sprinters. Less than a year before, on the powerful Nero, he had even established a new World record of nearly 110 mph over the measured kilometre from a standing-start.

So what was left? Almost everything, according to George. In spite of being 50 years old, he looked ambitiously to the future and to even more stirring deeds. But Nero was no longer the ultimate challenge. He needed a still more powerful machine, more potent, on which he could have a crack at the outright world record. That was his dearest ambition. Inspired by Britain's heritage in the four-wheel world through giants like John Cobb, Henry Segrave and, of course, Sir Malcolm Campbell, he saw the two-wheel 'world's fastest' as belonging to Britain, almost by divine right.

It was in 1962 that he talked seriously for the first time about a super-charged version of Nero as a machine which would bring him and Britain the World motor cycle land speed record. And in typical fashion, once the idea was lodged in his mind, he couldn't wait to turn the vision into reality. Incredibly, therefore, Super Nero was built that very same year. It would have been a massive challenge as a full-time project. It was little short of a miracle when you consider that most of the work had to be done at night, when the shop was shut and we could rid ourselves of the day-to-day selling, servicing and repairing of bikes from George's successful retail business.

We didn't make a start on Super Nero until after returning from the Isle of Man in June. In April and May George had shown his mastery by achieving

Fastest Time of the Day on Nero and leading the 250 cc field on the Ariel at the Pontypool sprint meeting in Wales. A couple of weeks later, at the Sunbeam Motor Cycle Club's meeting at Ramsgate — the first to be held there for nearly two years — he devastated all opposition, again being untouchable on the Ariel in the 250 cc class and holding off a supercharged challenge from the course record holder, Charlie Rous.

At Blackpool later that month he regained the course record, though his first run down the quarter mile strip in 11.89 seconds was 0.12 seconds slower than Charlie Rous's record of the previous year. But he made no mistake with his second run and secured the record with a tremendous ride in 11.37 seconds. During 1962 George netted 15 wins in hill climbs and sprints — more than enough for most sprinters but only sufficient to give grudging satisfaction to George. As I remember him saying to me at the time: *I ought to have done better than that* — though his record for the year worked out at a 90 per cent success rate, surely a sound enough performance in anybody's book.

In June we went to the Isle of Man to watch the races and George enjoyed meeting his old racing pals. He was thrilled that Geoff Duke invited him to display Nero in his showrooms at Douglas. The machine was spruced up and looked magnificent, drawing huge crowds. It was only when we were back in Stevenage after the TT that we began serious work on a supercharged version of Nero. The team was small but totally committed. In addition to George, who produced most of the basic ideas for his machines, there was Pat Barrett, no mean sprinter himself in the sidecar class, and myself, with George's wife Ada handling the paperwork, providing limitless cups of tea and coffee and — how she managed it all I'll never know — looking after their two sons, Antony and Graham. I was considered as occupying a key position in the project because of my experience in building Reg Dearden's ill-fated World's record challenger more than ten years before. Since 1973 the World's maximum speed record had been held by Germany and at the time, in 1950, stood to the credit of Ernst Henne at almost 174 mph. In March 1948 *The Motor Cycle* offered £500 to the first British rider on an all-British motor cycle to secure the official World's maximum motor cycle speed record. Encouraged by attempts by the Americans at Salt Lake, USA, Reg responded to the challenge and began the massive job of converting a standard production Vincent into a supercharged record-breaker. It was when he went out in search of help and Philip Vincent responded that I, then working for Vincent in the development department, was called in to do a considerable amount of work on the 998 cc Vincent Black Lightning which Reg had ordered for his basic machine. Some years later the machine had an extensive bottom-end rebuild with abnormally large main bearings and a prototype 'Picador' big end. It was a brave and expensive effort, but

Super Nero... view from the top. Picture taken just after building. Note the coils, positioned between the frame and the blow off valves from the supercharger. *(Motor Cycle Weekly)*

the purpose of it all — an attempt on the World record — never materialised and Reg later sold the machine.

I could well understand George's reasons for wanting a successor to Nero. Nero's engine had been tuned and developed to the ultimate and the standard Vincent Model C frame had been lowered and lightened, the wheelbase had been stretched to keep the front wheel from lifting high on take off, and Avon's slick rear tyre had just about eliminated wheelspin. Really, there was nowhere else to go with Nero. George now needed more power if he was to improve his performance and that meant a machine which could incorporate supercharging. His intention was to keep Nero for hill climbs and sprinting. Although we didn't announce it officially, George's idea with Super Nero was to produce a machine which, with the right level of development and supported by suitable sponsorship, would be capable of a serious attempt at the ultimate world title.

I got the wheels turning, so to speak, by getting Tim Hatton to cut a pattern of my blower plates out of three-ply wood, working from my drawings. In the meantime, George went to see Chris Shorrock and came back with a couple of mighty 1500 cc superchargers. We managed to get another Vincent engine and began building it up to the same standard as Nero, with two front cylinder heads, Picador-type ground flywheels assembly with 1 1/8 inch mainshafts, low compression pistons of 8 to 1, high-lift rockers and Stellite cam followers, which I ground on the lathe. With the engine assembled on the bench, George and I started to make the blower pipes to the cylinder heads from exhaust pipes and a silencer. Two safety valves were incorporated, one in each branch, and an extension on the pipes beyond the front branch was blanked off to ensure equal pressure distribution. At the end we also fitted a pipe for the boost gauge for the blow-off valves. Oil for the blower lubrication was carried in a small tank at the side of the gear change plate and was pressurised from the blower delivery side. We now took Nero's engine out of its frame and fitted the supercharged engine in its place, but we had to make a new seat frame to accommodate the blower. George bought new racing forks and a new front wheel from AJS and all we really used from Nero was the long swinging arm. We now fitted Nero's engine into another Vincent standard Model C frame and George was to go on using Nero in this form for another two years for hill climbs.

It is quite amazing when you consider that not many years later Honda would invest many thousands of pounds in the construction of their Hawk projectile in an unsuccessful bid to capture the World speed record. Yet here were George and I, with our backyard-type set-up, producing Super Nero on a budget which couldn't have topped £100, for the same purpose — and with the same disappointing results; though we did have the consolation of Super Nero's success as a sprint machine.

But in August 1962 we were full of hope as we took Super Nero down to Gransden Lodge for its first serious testing. It was cold, wet and windy as we pushed George off on his first trial run — Mr Irving, Pat Barrett, Tim Hatton, Ian Ashwell, George's son Antony, Vic Willoughby and myself. Certainly as dedicated a band of sprint enthusiasts as you are ever likely to see.

The bike was difficult to start at first and we traced the fault to weak carburation. SU Carburettors had fitted a number 2 needle, which was unsuitable for Super Nero, so as we only had a number 7 needle with us, I filed it down and by enriching the carburation we managed progressively to improve results during the hours before daylight faded.

Not a very auspicious baptism perhaps, but later that same month we blooded Super Nero at the National Sprint Association's Wellesbourne Mountford airfield meeting and George came away with the Fastest Time of the Day, though his 11.5 seconds was some way short of his standing figure on Nero. At Gransden we had found that the boost was not high enough and had fitted a 36-tooth sprocket on to the blower, but as the season developed we had to bring the blower pressure up again by fitting a 31-tooth sprocket. We also had quite a bit of trouble with magnetos misfiring due to the revs going so high that the winding insulation seemed to melt. We fitted a Scintilla magneto and that improved things. We were also troubled by breaking primary chains. Renolds were apparently having difficulty getting good carbon steel from Sweden and we were reduced to using standard chains. We went through them with alarming regularity! Little wonder, when you consider that Super Nero was developing 120 to 130 bhp, that we had to fit a new chain about every other meeting.

Two excellent meetings for Super Nero in this first year, however, were at Ramsgate and Duxford, both in the autumn. There were about 100 competitors at Ramsgate but George and Super Nero were the major attractions. George shattered the course record with a couple of runs at 11.55 seconds and a third at 11.59 secs, to take all the day's honours — the Record Cup, the Consistency Trophy and the Fastest Time of the Day. At Duxford, in spite of George being unwell, Super Nero was down to an astonishing 10.80 seconds — in spite of a nasty spasm of engine misfiring. There were other good performances during 1962 at Church Lawford, Tadcaster and Snetterton, and at Brighton where George recorded 20.8 seconds for the standing kilometre.

Super Nero's initiation had been one of motor cycle sport's major happenings in 1962. The machine, though carrying a lot of muscle, was easier to ride and George was having to get used to a new riding technique. As he told a national newspaper reporter: *Old Nero was a bit brutal at certain speeds and took a lot of handling. Now I'm having to learn to ride all over again because this one (Super Nero) hums along like a Cadillac.* Most important of all, the new machine had produced a number of good results and many encouraging performances.

So into 1963 — a hectic year with no fewer than 14 sprint meetings for Nero and Super Nero, and three major hill climbs at Wiscombe Park, Shelsley Walsh and at Cork in Northern Ireland. When George travelled to Cork, the Irish record for the standing kilometre stood to Charlie Rous, with 21.7 seconds recorded two years before. But George took Super Nero down the famous Carrigrohane Straight to cover the distance in an impressive 19.4 seconds. It was not only good enough to take the Irish record from Charlie officially, but the time was an unofficial World record for the distance. George was jubilant and at the same time annoyed with himself because he reckoned he had misjudged the conditions and consequently Super Nero had been undergeared. *Otherwise I'd have done better,* he said. He was clocking about 185 mph at the end of the kilometre. With the correct gearing, he could have expected his terminal speed to be nearer 220 mph. His average was 114.8 mph. The first run, made against a strong three-quarter wind, took 19.36 seconds, but a below-standard start on the return run dropped Super Nero down to 19.5 seconds. Yet the performance was good enough for him to make Fastest Time of the Day.

The very next day George exchanged Super Nero for Nero and triumphed again, this time in the second leg of the Munster Club's Speed Weekend, the Farnanes hill climb. He blasted Nero up in 1 minute 23.4 seconds to beat the existing record by almost ten seconds. Later in the year George enhanced his reputation as perhaps the country's most successful hill climber with another staggering performance at the famous Shelsley Walsh meeting. He took both the 350 cc and 1000 cc results and *Motorcycle Sport* were moved to pay this fine tribute to George's skill up the hills: *Mr Brown, obviously, was aware of the bends in the Shelsley gradient, but he didn't allow the bends to influence him a great deal: he acknowledged their existence by changing gear once or twice and leaning Nero this way and that, and pressed on to the top. He found grip in the wet where others were wobbling, refused to lower a foot or elevate an elbow and thundered on purposefully and very rapidly. His first time was 42.66 seconds, the 65th (or thereabouts) time recorded that day and the best by nearly 2 seconds. Later he did 41.78 seconds.* That was a nice tribute which George appreciated.

Super Nero under assembly in 1963. *(Motor Cycle Weekly)*

At home at Shelsley in 1964. *(Guy Griffiths)*

On Ramsgate's narrow promenade, George and Super Nero chopped almost half a second off the absolute record with an 11.08 seconds performance, but in 1963 Brighton was undoubtedly the highlight, for it was at the South Coast resort that George became the fastest man in the world to cover a kilometre from a standing start with any machine, four-wheeled or two. He went to Brighton with a previous best of 20.99 seconds, but his shattering performance in 1963 clipped more than 1½ seconds off that time. With an average speed of 117 mph and a terminal speed of 186 mph, George completed a run of 19.29 seconds to win, as I have already mentioned, two of Bemsee's highest awards, the Silver Star and the double Gold Star, for an average speed in excess of 115 mph.

It was rather surprising in 1964 that the current British National record for the flying start kilometre had stood for so long. But as George travelled to Chelveston Airfield in Northamptonshire in June that year he was determined to add that particular distinction to his growing list of triumphs, as well as making a bid for a number of world records. Conditions were far from perfect with a strong, gusty wind proving troublesome, but George elected to go first for the Flying Kilometre National Record. This had been set by Londoner Joe Wright who, in 1930, had gained immortality by taking a 998 cc OEC Temple JAP to Cork in Ireland and capturing the outright World record from Germany's Ernst Henne at a speed of 150.5 mph. That same year he had set the British National flying kilometre record on a 995 cc Zenith at 151 mph, but George was confident he could do better and with the rear wheel spinning frantically, he was soon off, rocketing through the electronic timing gear to record a first run speed of 181.66 mph. His return run was much less good, but the average of 172.70 mph was more than enough to give him the National record and set him up for more success to come.

The surface of Chelveston's two mile runway was coated with smooth asphalt and it was just too slippery for George to go seriously for any standing quarter mile attempts on that day. The grip on take off simply wasn't good enough, but for the fun of it he made a few runs and in typically disarming fashion, knocked over a second off his own World and National kilometre times. The first runs, with a 42 tooth rear sprocket, produced times of 19.82 seconds and 19.67 seconds for a mean 19.75 seconds, or 113 mph. This was well in keeping with the one per cent improvement required under FIM regulations for a new time to count as a record. Though it was good enough for the authorities, George wasn't really satisfied, so I fitted a 40 tooth rear sprocket and George went away again. He got his times down to 19.37 and 19.58 (mean 19,48 seconds), to give a new speed of 114 mph, to break his previous unblown record handsomely for both a new World and National record.

George was smiling now and much more satisfied. His next objective was the National flying quarter mile record, but the weather was deteriorating so we abandoned record breaking until the next day. In the meantime I changed the rear slick tyre to a normal road racing type and fitted a gasket to the timing gear, which was leaking. Sunday dawned brighter and as the weather cleared, George swept Super Nero into action, establishing a new National flying-start quarter mile record, his best run equalling 187 mph. In doing so he ran off line and clouted an airfield landing light, denting Super Nero's front wheel, and on his third run he missed the timing gear completely, the wind was so strong. On his next two runs George had to lean well out of the fairing as the strong wind threatened to take charge on westerly runs, but his mean speed was still 177.2 mph. This had been an exhilarating weekend with superb dashes and with as much of the traditional action of sprint as one could wish for — exciting getaways on the gravel surface, plenty of wheelspin and over-revving, and a superb demonstration of riding as George struggled to hold Super Nero firm against the insistent cross wind.

George had no real cause to complain. With four new records in the bag, and the distinction of now being the fastest man timed in Britain on any

More record attempts at Chelveston. *(Motor Cycle Weekly)*
Nero travelling at 280 feet per second ... too fast for the camera.

wheeled vehicle, who could begrudge him his few defiant words as he departed Chelveston. *Now pick the bones out of that,* was all he said.

Here is a summary of George's records at Chelveston that weekend:
WORLD RECORD
Standing-start kilometre: 1000 cc, 114.83 mph, 19.48 seconds (Super Nero)
BRITISH RECORDS
Standing-start kilometre: Details as above
Flying-start kilometre: 1000 cc, 172.7 mph, 12.96 seconds (Super Nero)
Flying-start quarter mile: 1000 cc, 177.16 mph, 5.08 seconds (Super Nero)

But of course, a mere recital of runs and speeds conveys nothing of the style and brilliance with which George performed these stirring deeds. It would be easy, and perhaps forgiveable, for his brother to become over-emotional about George's achievements. So let's see what the old weekly *The Motor Cycle* said about the Chelveston weekend. This respected magazine described his performances as ... *a series of solo dashes more brilliant and courageous than he has ever made* ... and concluded the report in this vein: *George waited patiently for the strip to dry, then reeled off those magnificent flying quarters* ...

If Thurleigh had been available that particular weekend there is no doubt that George's performance would have been better, even if not more impressive. Because of Chelveston's less charitable surface on that occasion, it required all George's skill and experience to coax those exceptional runs from Super Nero. With the rear wheel so prone to spin, careful throttle control off the line was essential. Even in such an impressive weekend of record breaking George found time to ride the 750 cc supercharged BSA sprinter which Geoff Garside of BSA had brought along in the hope that he would not only ride it, but go for a number of records. Although it never really came to anything because the engine persisted in firing on only one cylinder, George did a very creditable 14.02 seconds for the quarter, in spite of the BSA's bent pushrod and broken rocker.

Altogether, George did 15 sprint meetings with Super Nero in 1964 and at the Duxford Kilometre Meeting he succeeded with a time of 18.90 seconds one way, thus unofficially breaking his own World record. We went back to Chelveston twice that year in an attempt to better existing records. George was in scintillating form in August and after being up with the lark, chopped some twelve miles an hour off his own record for the flying quarter with some fantastic runs ... before breakfast! His fastest one way run at 4.714 seconds gave him a speed of 190.92 mph. He was pulling a 3.5 to 1 top gear to stop wheelspin and over-revving on the dust and sand. After he had snaked Super Nero through the stretch of very rough loose sand and gravel which extended for about three hundred yards at each end of the measured distance, George settled the machine down to a series of rock steady runs. It was after I had changed the needle on the SU carburettor as the mixture was slightly rich, and at the end of a return run had fixed a rubber band on to a rear brake return spring which had broken, that the record was in the bag. We rested during the heat of the day, but in the evening George got busy again, although the wind was rising. His target this time was the standing quarter mile and he cut his own record time for this to a mean 10.283 seconds, which compared with his old record set on the unblown Nero at Thurleigh of 10.49 seconds.

Results
National 1000 cc flying-start quarter mile
First run: 4.714 seconds, 190.92 mph
Second run: 4.754 seconds, 187.774 mph
Mean: 4.374 seconds, 189.314 mph.
National 1000 cc standing-start quarter mile
First run: 10.167 seconds
Second run: 10.399 seconds
Mean: 10.283 seconds.

Ready for the record, note the 136lbs of lead ballast subsitute for passenger.

During George's day there had always been keen rivalry between the British and American sprinters, fuelled I'm sure by reports and rumours about some remarkable performances supposedly having been completed on the other side of the Atlantic. Some, certainly, were treated with a good deal of scepticism in Britain, so when at the end of 1962 the Americans offered a challenge to George to take a three-man team over there and compete against the best Americans, he not only got excited at the prospect from a personal standpoint (he always had difficulty in side-stepping a challenge), but he considered it a genuine opportunity to put British sprinting on the world map. He was sure the old country could put up a good performance and in no time had settled on his team — himself on Super Nero, Charlie Rous on Nero and Alf Hagon on the two-speed Triumph 650.

Unfortunately the challenge never materialised, but the American dragsters did come over to Britain when the National Sprint Association, in conjunction with the British Drag Association, invited the American Drag Association to a drag festival for both cars and motor cycles at a series of meetings held at six airfields. They came in 1964, but before the Americans settled down to their British competition programme, they went to the Continent to give a number of demonstrations of drag racing in Italy. This enterprising move came from the National Sprint Association secretary Len Cole, who used to travel to Italy buying Lambretta spares for his wholesale firm. Len also arranged for George to go to Italy at the same time as the Americans and he, George and young Antony formed the British contingent, along with Dr Bayley, the National Sprint Association medical man. He took my place because George thought it would be useful to have a qualified doctor in the party, and he said he would be happier if I stayed at home to help his wife Ada look after the shop.

Destination for George and his party and the Americans was the famous Monza circuit. The Italians had heard of drag racing, but had never seen it, so the occasion included a number of demonstration runs. The Americans didn't have much luck, blowing up a lot of their car engines, but George became an unqualified hero, with the Italians calling for more and more of the George Brown action. He completed a number of really impressive runs and his courage and exceptional mastery of Super Nero were widely acclaimed. The Italians not only responded to the spectacle of it all, but loved George for calling his bike Super Nero. Because of the Latin association, they accepted him as a special friend and gave him twelve bottles of their finest wine to bring home.

This Italian venture was also remembered by George for another less rewarding incident. On their way to Italy the party made good progress through France and over the Alps, but shortly after crossing into Italy they came across a roundabout and motored round it the English way. They were nabbed by the police and each fined the nominal sum of one thousand lire. The police wouldn't allow them to proceed until they had paid the fine on the spot.

At this point George and Super Nero were the most exciting, prolific and dominant sprint and record breaking combination in the country, but for the Drag Festival with the Americans, to which George was committed later in the year, Super Nero in her then present form would be out of her element. That's why George and I set to work on some essential modifications. We made a new rigid frame of 5/8 inch 531 tubing, in order to get the bike nearer to the ground. George bought some 70 cc Honda forks, which were very light, and a 17 inch front wheel. We shortened the front forks by an inch. I had a slave engine which I put on the work bench with a 2 inch block of wood underneath. The head lug was 2 inch diameter drilled and turned inside to fit the Honda fork ballraces, with the front forks and front wheel set up to a 30 degree angle. With brackets welded to the 5/8 inch tubing, the frame was ready to be welded to the head lug. It shows how 'part time' the whole preparations were when I explain that George welded the frame in between looking after the shop.

First tryout of the new frame was at the NSA Debden Airfield sprint in Essex and all went very well. George raced away in a straight line and made Fastest Time of the Day. We declared our work and the new frame an outright success.

We had to discard the Vincent oil tank for the new frame and we used the gearbox for the oil tank to feed the engine. George had a small fuel tank made in aluminium to lie on. I dismantled the engine to make sure everything was in order and after I had rebuilt it we were ready for the series of drag meetings with the Americans.

Speed king George Brown (right) receives the Pepsi-Cola Trophy at the first Drag Festival prize giving in 1964.

For all George had become a king in the purist sphere of sprinting he accepted drag racing reasonably readily and was soon applying his energies and ingenuity to beating the Americans at their own game. At Blackbushe at the first meeting he recorded times of 11.28 seconds and 11.64 seconds to make the Fastest Time of the Day, well ahead of the Americans, in spite of a misfiring magneto on Super Nero. New points and a new condenser failed to cure the misfiring, and the engine would not rev, so George was able to make no impression at all at the second encounter at Chelveston. I found that the blower had sheared, so a new blower was fitted for the third meeting at RAF Woodvale. Still the magneto misfired, but George worked so well that he was able to make fastest time with runs of 10.75 and 10.89 seconds. I missed the Woodvale meeting, but George rang through to the shop to tell me to take the magneto out of Nero and get it up to Church Fenton, near York, in double quick time ready for the next meeting. I drove up there like a maniac in George's Mini and soon had the new magneto fitted neatly into Super Nero. It did the trick and George was back among the results. He was also unbeatable at the final two meetings in the series, recording times of 10.37, 10.30, 10.77 and 10.49 seconds. The Americans were beaten by the British NSA riders and George finished the series with five outstanding wins out of a possible six — not bad going for someone moving towards his middle fifties.

It was a fitting climax to the season when George and I attended a special function at a hotel in London's Park Lane as guests of the Americans. George received no fewer than five gold cups for his remarkable catalogue of wins and was acclaimed by the American motor cycle press as the 'father of sprinting'. I was also surprised and delighted when I was called to the stage to be presented with a gold plated torque wrench by the American Drag Association for preparing the most successful bike and being the most successful mechanic of the whole festival.

Chapter 9

Great Days at Greenham Common

NOT EVEN George had an answer to the passing of time and in 1965 he was 53. At 55, in just two years' time, it would be necessary for him to retire officially from International record breaking. That was the ruling established and upheld by the FIM. Not just for George. For everyone.

George hated the idea of growing too old to race. For a long time he pushed it to the back of his mind. When he saw the age barrier in view, he had a final, official, defiant fling. Then he embarked on an active and sustained campaign to get the rule changed. And won!

In the meantime his ambition, among all kinds of other records, was to be the first man to travel at 200 mph on a motor cycle on British soil. We'd planned that for 1966 so while we prepared one of the biggest programmes of George's entire career, we had a relatively quiet — for George — year in 1965. Even so he rode at eleven meetings, including seven at Duxford, the Isle of Man, Swinderby, Poddington and Debden. In 1965 I completely dismantled Super Nero's engine. We bolted the two crankcases together and had the case bored out, fitting steel housings for the main bearings. Then the mouth of the crankcase was bored out 95 mm so that we could convert the 1000 cc engine into a 1148 cc unit. I had two sleeves made for the barrel mouths so that all I had to do was to take the sleeves out or put them back in to make the bike 1000 cc or 1148 cc, also by exchanging the barrels and fitting Matchless G50 racing pistons. George had a twin points coil ignition system made and we first tried this out at Swinderby as a 1000 cc unit, but the rear conrods broke, damaging the crankcase, barrels and pistons. I then assembled a standard 1000 cc crankcase with steel main bearings housings only, with a new set of flywheels, barrels and pistons. We tried this out at

Debden, but the bike misfired badly, so I changed the carb needle, checked the points, and fitted a Honda coil. It did the trick because at the next meeting, at Duxford, George was successful.

It was at this meeting that we discovered by chance why the bikes were always misfiring with coil ignition. Because of the vibration, the plates in the two batteries which were fitted at the back under the gearbox broke up inside, so from then on we always carried two spare batteries whenever we went sprinting.

It was before the start of the 1966 season that George and I set about building a Super Nero Mark 2, with a 1148 cc engine. The frame was identical to that of Super Nero Mark 1. We now had two supercharged bikes we could take to a meeting, lessening George's vulnerability if the original Super Nero became temperamental. For Mark 2 I made a special two-speed gearbox which could easily be changed into a four-speed, and altogether it was as hectic a time as we could remember as we prepared for a gruelling and highly expectant 1966 season.

In recognition of George's contribution to motor cycle sport over a number of years he had been made an honorary member of the RAF Motor Sport Association and was now so well respected that he had only to ask for the use of a suitable airfield for permission to be given, almost as a formality. He had Greenham Common airfield, near Newbury in Berkshire, in mind for his next important record breaking attempts and he and helper/enthusiast Mick Fraser went there to give it the once-over. It was about now that George parted company after many years of success with his Ariel racer. The factory was on the point of closing, so George off-loaded the bike and all its spares to an NSA club member and bought two Royal Enfield engines from Geoff Duke, which Geoff Duke's riders had used in the TTs. For the new engine we built a special sprint frame.

George had booked Greenham Common for October 5/6/7/8 and we took a mass of machinery, equipment, spares and 'support' engines with us. The RAF did us proud. They let us use their workshops and housed us in the Officers' Mess, with heated radiators, wash basins with hot and cold water, showers, and camp beds. Reveille was fixed for 4.30 am, so we turned in early, intending to get a good night. Almost immediately, an enormous crash roused us as the camp bed on which Tony Driscoll, one of our team, was sleeping collapsed and we had to pick him up off the floor from among the woodworm. Once we had organised him again with a hastily repaired bed built up with the aid of books, we all settled down once more ... only to discover that nobody had bothered to put the lights out. Philip, a friend of Antony's who had come along for the ride, was detailed to get up and switch off the light. Only then did we get some sleep.

Dead on 4.30 am I was awakened by the delicious smell of bacon and

The lonely world of the record breaker. George at Greenham Common in 1966. *(Herts Pictorial)*

No records today. Greenham Common in 1966 with the 'wind machine' in the foreground proving that the wind is too strong for attempts to be made. *(Motor Cycle Weekly)*

eggs and the sight of irrepressible George cooking breakfast for the entire party.

There was an atmosphere of expectancy in our small, enthusiastic party, but on that first morning visibility was down to 150 yeards and we all waited impatiently hoping for the weather to clear. The authorities had done all they could to help us, allocating the bottom area of the control tower for a trackside workshop and the tarmac layby as a car park for the Castrol vans and sundry other vehicles. But not until the afternoon were we able to wheel out the 250 cc Royal Enfield for George to run the standing quarter mile in a very stiff breeze. It was positively unsafe for any serious runs with the larger machines . . . even with the streamlining removed. It was a miserable first day and at the end of it only one record had been taken, the 250 cc World standing quarter mile at 14.842 seconds (60.639 mph). Thursday was even more desperate, rain permitting only a couple of runs all day and these again on the 250 cc machine. But somehow George managed to hoist the record to 62.15 mph before the clutch started to give trouble and the bike had to be wheeled back into the workshop for essential attention.

Friday provided the best weather yet and for the first time George hoped to get down to some really serious record breaking. With the Royal Enfield he pushed the standing quarter up another fraction, to 62.639 mph, and at noon George decided to bring out Super Nero . . . just as the French FIM steward Jacques Renoult shocked everyone by announcing that he was ready to go home that evening and no records could therefore be attempted on the Saturday. As I wrote in Chapter Two, part of Friday was wasted while George pleaded with him, insisting he was booked to stay there over Saturday. He made a number of frantic calls to Paris which finally provided George with the news he wanted and he was able to confirm that the arrangements were for the Frenchman to stay at Greenham Common on Saturday.

By now it was too late to do any fast runs with the big bikes, so George contented himself by breaking his old Ariel Arrow flying start kilometre record with runs at 17.890 and 18.646 seconds to give an average of 18.268 seconds (122.451 mph), against the old record of 106.7 mph. It was now so late in the day that George took his new record with the all the headlights of the cars lined up down the runway to show him the way through the speed trap and the finishing point. It was fish and chips and beer for supper, an early night, and another 4.30 am rise on Saturday. After three disappointing, wearisome and costly days of mist, rain and high winds, Saturday dawned perfect and George couldn't wait to get started. The state of the run way, however, robbed him of any chance of going for the flying records on the big machines and so, for the time being, his chance of becoming the first man to crack the 200 mph barrier on a motor cycle on British soil before he was 55 had to be abandoned. Twice he beat his own World and National

George's naked Royal Enfield at Greenham Common, 1966. *(Motor Cycle Weekly)*

Super Nero naked at Greenham Common. *(Motor Cycle Weekly)*

standing-start kilometre 1000 cc runs, but not by the necessary one per cent margin. Then George showed his outstanding talent and resilience and in spite of his bitter disappointments over the previous three days, record after record fell to him on the final day, converting in a few hours a series of dismal failures into a period of dazzling success.

But he was showing signs of strain after such a hectic time and was considerably bruised from the constant hammering of his rigid framed machines as he rocketed up and down the disused airstrip.

A rundown on the day and its achievements goes like this:

Standing-start kilometre   (Solo) 1000 cc   (World & British National)
Mean Time 19.15 secs   Average speed 116.79 mph (Old record 114.83 mph)
Standing-start kilometre   (Sidecar) 1000 cc   (World & British National)
Mean Time 21.92 secs   Average speed 102.01 mph
Standing-start ¼ mile   (Sidecar) 1000 cc   (World & British National)
Mean Time 11.80 secs   Average speed 76.22 mph
Standing-start ¼ mile   (Solo) 1300 cc   (British National)
Mean Time 11.13 secs   Average speed 80.84 mph
Flying-start kilometre   250 cc Royal Enfield Special   (British National)
Mean Time 18.26 secs   Average speed 122.45 mph (Old record 106.7 mph)
Standing-start kilometre 250 cc Royal Enfield Special   (British National)
Mean Time 26.89 secs   Average speed 83.18 mph   (Old record 77.5 mph)
Standing-start ¼ mile   250 cc Royal Enfield Special   (World record)
Mean Time 14.49 secs   Average speed 62.63 mph (Old record 58.31 mph)

Weather Conditions

Wednesday 5th October:	Visibility down to 150 yards prevented any morning runs.
Thursday 6th October:	Persistent rain all day stopped any serious record attempts.
Friday 7th October:	High winds gusting up to 15 knots across the runway together with very low temperatures made runs dangerous.
Saturday 8th October:	Bad visibility prevented very early morning runs; almost all the records above were done in the short time of five hours.

Although in the circumstances George had achieved more than could have been expected of him at Greenham Common, his four days there hadn't brought the success he had hoped for, so instead of attending the NSA World record breaking weekend at Elvington, near York, we stayed at Stevenage preparing to go back to Greenham Common for a three-day session in early November, just three months before his 55th birthday, after which he would be too old for further World record attempts under the FIM's present ruling.

Chapter 9/113

Plenty of work for George, Cliff and (centre) Bob Slater. *(Motor Cycle Weekly)*

I got down to the job of modifying the frames and engines of both the big bikes, building spare rear wheels with slick tyres and high speed tyres to save time when changing them. Then off we went again to Greenham Common, hell-bent on bringing back the records we had missed out on a month before. It was to be a sensational occasion with George proving beyond doubt that he was the world's master sprinter. He shattered record after record, many of which had been set up only days before at the NSA weekend at Elvington. With terminal speeds approaching 200 mph solo and 180 mph sidecar, George cracked some records by astonishing margins of over 20 mph — all officially observed by the Polish FIM Vice President, Bogden Matuszak and the A-CU's John McNulty, in weather ranging from sunshine to snowstorms.

George was totally irrepressible. Because of the FIM's age barrier he expected this to be his final fling and he went out in a blaze of glory, adding seven World and nine British sprint records to his collection of over 30. From the start he was devastating, warming up by establishing a record for the 1300 cc solo standing-start mile with an average of 28.032 seconds (128 mph), nine miles an hour faster than Ian Ashwell's record breaking performance at Elvington in October. We then fitted the sidecar with its 132 lb of lead ballast to the 1000 cc machine and George made a series of dazzling runs over the standing mile, this time averaging 30.346 seconds (119.087 mph), to shatter Vic Phillips' Impetus time by 22 miles an hour. The next day George added the 1300 cc sidecar standing-start mile to his tally at a slightly slower speed of 31.057 seconds (115.916 mph).

The original 1000 cc Super Nero was proving faster than its bigger brother. With it George shattered Eric Fernihough's old sidecar flying kilometre record of 1937 by 21 miles an hour, setting the new figure at 158.23 mph, and even as darkness fell and snow swept across the airfield, George took the 1300 cc Super Nero Mark 2 to a new record over the sidecar flying kilometre. He bettered Maurice Brierley's previous record by 11 miles an hour, setting a new time of 14.939 seconds and a new speed of 149.732 mph.

Fog and frost delayed the start on Friday, but the sun came through mid-morning and George was away again. With the 1300 cc machine he captured the sidecar standing start kilometre record at 21.625 seconds (103.439 mph). It was now so cold that the carburettors were icing up, but George wouldn't be stopped. With the 1000 cc machine he tried to improve on his own solo standing start kilometre record, but the bike slipped out of gear on the return run. With strong winds imminent he switched to the 1300 cc sidecar outfit and two more records fell. Still he wasn't satisfied and in one impressive final dash over the flying quarter mile, not recognised by the FIM, he raised the British record by no less than 24 miles an hour.

Chapter 9/115

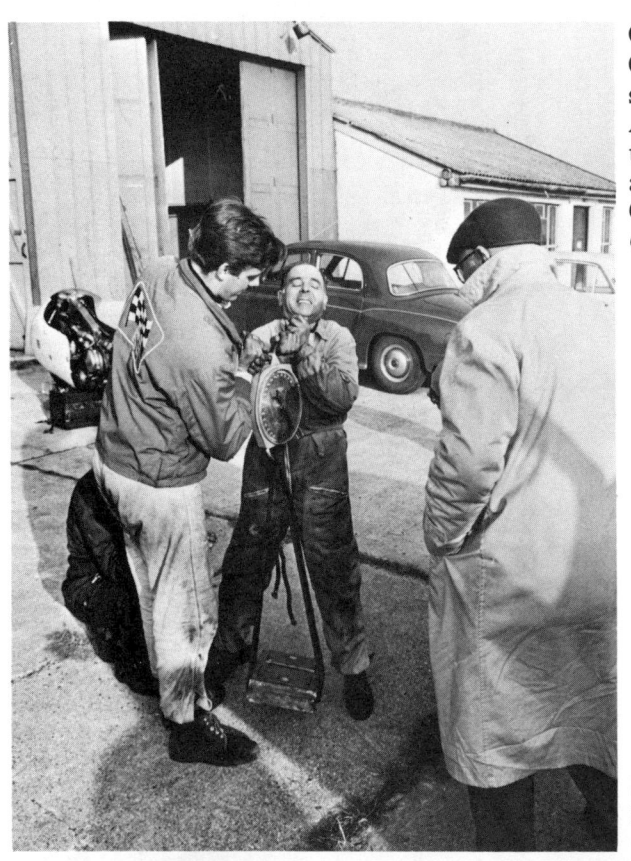

George's son Antony and Cliff Brown check the sidecar weight with an A-CU official ready for the record breaking attempts at Greenham Common in 1966. *(Motor Cycle Weekly)*

Super Nero with sidecar in October 1966. *(G. Gredwell)*

George and Mick Fraser deal with Nero's broken chain. *(Motor Cycle Weekly)*

George, with Mick Fraser and son Antony, filling Super Nero. *(Motor Cycle Weekly)*

The Royal Enfield, smooth in streamlining, at Greenham Common. *(Motor Cycle Weekly)*
George at speed on the Royal Enfield at Greenham Common in 1966. *(Motor Cycle Weekly)*

George travelling at speed on Super Nero. Note the way the bike leans because of the wind. *(D. J. Dixon)*

Starting technique for a monster. Power from the van spins the rear wheel of Super Nero via rollers. *(Motor Cycle Weekly)*

Cliff cleaning Super Nero after a run at Greenham Common in 1966. *(Herts Pictorial)*

The correct position means everything. George's record breaking technique as he attacks the sidecar records.

George was all set to attack at least another four records when timekeeper Vic Anstic, compelled to leave for another appointment, called a halt.

It had been three days of phenomenal record breaking — George at his dazzling best — and after it was all over he relaxed and wisecracked, telling *Motor Cycle News's* Peter Howdle: *My 55th birthday is on February 22nd, but I intend going to Nottingham to make sure the registrar didn't make a mistake. I think the FIM age ruling for sprinting is a lot of boloney. Don't be surprised if I have another go before February 21st.*

His complete dossier of record breaking at Greenham Common on 3rd, 4th and 5th November 1966 was as follows:

Standing-start mile (Solo) 1300 cc (World & British National)
Mean Time 31.366 secs   Average speed 114 mph   (Old record 105.67 mph)
Standing-start mile (Solo) 1000 cc (World & British National)
Mean Time 28.032 secs   Average speed 128.46 mph   (Old record 97.32 mph)
Standing-start mile (Sidecar) 1000 cc (World & British National)
Mean Time 30.446 secs   Average speed 119.086 mph (Old record 105.67 mph)
Flying-start kilometre (Sidecar) 1000 cc (World & British National)
Mean Time 14.112 secs   Average speed 158.238 mph
Standing-start mile (Sidecar) 1300cc (World & British National)
Mean Time 31.057 secs   Average speed 115.915 mph
Flying-start kilometre (Sidecar) 1300 cc (World & British National)
Mean Time 14.939 secs   Average speed 149.732 mph
Standing-start kilometre (Sidecar) 1300 cc (World & British National)
Mean Time 21.625 secs   Average speed 103.439 mph   (Old record 97.20 mph)
Flying-start ¼ mile (Sidecar) 1300 cc (British National only)
Mean Time 5.888 secs   Average speed 152.840 mph (Old record 128.72 mph)
Standing start mile   250 cc Royal Enfield Special   (British National)
Mean Time 37.392 secs   Average speed 96.404 mph

Due to weather variables, (early morning frost, bad visibility, extreme low temperatures, wind speed above the normal safety margin) it was agreed with the officials that any attempts on the flying solo distances would be too dangerous. Fastest one-way speed with sidecar machines was 166.57 mph. During the combined attempts no fewer than eleven World records were taken and sixteen British National records, despite bad weather conditions.

Mechanically, the three days at Greenham Common were punishing, but we had no engine failures. Our main problem came from chain breakages on the 1148 cc machine, due to the bike's power. George and I put this down to whip on the new frame, so we welded an extra tube to the rear of the frame; but a fifth chain broke almost immediately and by this time we had also smashed three gearboxes. I had only one set of gearbox internals left and they were in Nero, so out they had to come. By now I was beginning to

George's many successes were always the result of a team effort. Left to right: (front) George, Mick Fraser, Antony, and Tony Driscoll; (back) Cliff, George Hall and Brian Young.

doubt if Renold had supplied us with racing chains, as they should have done, so before letting George ride the bike again, I decided we ought to use the old racing chains from the 1960 record breaking session. Brian Young, a Stevenage Club member, was despatched to Stevenage. On his return I fitted the old chains and we had no further trouble. So I proved the point that Renold had supplied us with standard commercial chains and they later paid for three sets of Vincent gearbox internals.

Chapter 10

Magnificent Elvington

IN 1967 George had celebrated his 55th birthday and his application to go for a number of international records at Elvington that year was turned down by the FIM. The occasion was to be an exciting weekend of record breaking by Britain's superstars of sprinting like Fred Cooper, Alf Hagon, Des Heckle, Owen Greenwood and others, and organised by the International Sprint Organisation. Altogether 89 World and National sprint records were secured for Britain during the speed marathon weekend. George was in typically defiant mood, responding in characteristic style to the FIM refusal to allow him to go for World records. On the 1300 cc Super Nero he did the standing-start mile in 27.96 seconds (128.7 mph) and the flying-start kilometre in 13.03 seconds (171.68 mph). Both runs were better than the then existing World records set up the year before, but because George was over 55, they could only count as new British National records.

George wasn't the type to give way to emotional outbursts, but I could see he was disappointed to be denied official 'World' recognition for his record breaking runs. On the other hand he found a kind of 'I told you so' satisfaction in demonstrating that even at 55 he was still fit and expert enough to crack World records . . . certainly out on the strip if not in the official record books. And he was proud of son Antony's performance. Going for the standing-start quarter mile on Super Nero, Tony travelled east to west on his first run in 12.864 seconds. He reduced that time on the return run to 12.642 seconds, to give a mean 12.753 seconds. On these two runs he had used only third and top gear, but his times for his second runs using all three gears and a 25 per cent nitro mixture, were down to a mean 11.836 seconds. As he prepared for his third attempt a new record looked a possibility. Using the same set-up he made east to west in 11.884 and west to east in 11.648 to give a mean time of 11.746. It was enough to give Antony Brown a World and British National record and at 20 years of age he was the youngest official World record holder in sprinting, not only in Britain but throughout the world. It was a proud moment for us all.

The latter part of 1967 and the early part of 1968 were significant times for the Brown family. George's sprinting activities were curtailed because of increasing business at the shop and his record breaking drive had lost some of its edge because of the FIM's age ban which put paid to his International record breaking. We were all saddened when my father, a day or two after his 79th birthday, was admitted to hospital and died a few days later, on November 6th. It seemed to close a chapter in our lives because through all George's long career in motor cycling, dad had been present and was extremely proud of what both George and I had achieved in the motor cycle world. He had always encouraged us and had been a constant source of inspiration. We were fortunate that both mother and father had always taken an active interest in what George and I had done — always being present at race meetings in their familiar old Ford Anglia. They were always thrilled and proud when we had a success. And of course it was through their devotion to motor cycles that George and I had become interested as lads. It was a sad time. For me, also, domestic problems came to a head and my wife and I separated, some years later to be divorced. I met my second wife, Doreen, when she came into George's shop to buy a P50 Honda moped with the engine in the back wheel. She later came back, complaining about it seizing up. When I discovered that she had ridden to Windsor and back accompanying her brother, who was riding a much more powerful bike, and had tried to keep up with him, I gave her a straight lesson in the responsible and sensible treatment of motor cycles. Two years later we were married.

In 1967 we also experienced an unusual number of mechanical problems. Duxford was something of a jinx course. At our first meeting there that year, Super Nero's drive shaft broke on the Shorrocks' blower. At the second meeting the crank pin broke on the drive side and smashed the crankcase beyond repair. This was on top of a problem meeting at Ramsgate when the second gear pinion and double gear smashed and I had to fit a new high bottom and second gear. But the period had its happier moments and George was able to enjoy some well earned glory when he was invited to the Kirkistown short circuit road race meeting promoted by the Belfast and District Motor Club to give a demonstration on Super Nero.

George wasn't prepared to accept the FIM's age embargo on his record attempts and wrote direct to their headquarters in Geneva, Switzerland, explaining that although he was 55 he was perfectly fit, had a clean record of health from his doctors and was probably better able, physically, to go for

International records at 55 years of age than many others who were ten years younger. What maddened George most perhaps was the incongruous situation which officially recognised him fit enough to tackle British National records on Brighton promenade, where there were lamp standards, railings and all sorts of hazards, but denied him the chance to go for World records on long, unimpeded aircraft runways with more than two miles of concrete to run on.

He also pointed out the possibility of a rather ludicrous situation developing. Because of George's success we were already getting to the stage where British National records could be better than the World equivalent. George was determined to continue to improve National records, as he was perfectly entitled to do under the National Auto-Cycle Union regulations, so if this trend continued, the World records were bound to lose authority and credibility. George lost no opportunity in pointing all this out to the FIM and by the middle of 1968 they relented and lifted the 55 year old age limit, much to our delight.

The Elvington record weekend was coming up and, inspired by the FIM's 'go-ahead' decision, George was filled with enthusiasm once more. I prepared both bikes, as both George and Antony were to compete. George started in phenomenal style. He decided to take Super Nero out for the flying-start quarter mile — *just as a run in* — he told me; but with hardly any preparation his first run was timed at 5.287 seconds — equivalent to an astonishing 170.4 mph. The bike was going so well that he immediately turned Super Nero round and opened up the throttle again, completing the return run in 5.132 seconds (175 mph). His mean time was 5.209 seconds, an average of 175 mph, and good enough for a new British National record. More than that, he had become the fastest man in Europe on two wheels, unofficially, by crossing the terminal marker of the two mile course travelling at 236 mph.

The next day (Sunday) George took a World and National record with a brilliant flying kilometre performance. On the outward run the sprinters were handicapped by having only about 400 yards in which to pull up at the end of the measured distance, but in spite of this George still managed to clock 12.656 seconds (175 mph). On the return run he really made the dust fly, getting the time down to 11.685 seconds, an average of 189 mph. The two runs' mean time was an incredible 12.285 seconds, 182 mph. Overall it was a remarkable performance and George was presented with a special shield by one of the sponsoring companies and christened the King of Speed, a very appropriate accolade, and an honour he richly deserved. Evidence of George's demands on Super Nero was the condition of the back tyre after the last two runs. It was worn through to the canvas.

It was a very successful meeting for the Stevenage Club. Antony, riding

Super Nero I in sidecar form, completed his runs for the flying-start quarters at an average of 6.135 seconds (146.7 mph) for a new British National record. Although on the outward run on the flying mile he clocked 24.810 seconds (144.96 mph), he was to be dogged by bad luck on his return runs. On his first return a wire came off the coil. He went for a complete re-run and improved his outward run speed to 23.394 seconds (153.96 mph), and with the World record standing at only 119 mph he could cruise home on the return run and still make it with plenty of mph in hand. But this time the primary chain broke and jammed, smashing the gearbox and crankcase, and by the time Super Nero came to rest on the grass the back tyre had worn through to the inner tube and the front brake was smoking. But Antony also bettered existing National records for three other runs — the standing mile, standing quarter and the flying quarter mile for sidecars.

Elvington was the venue at which George's career was effectively to end. In 1970 he roared back after many relatively quiet months and at the pre-records day meeting in September set fastest speeds in both solo and sidecar classes on his 1,000 cc Super Nero. With sidecar attached he swept through the timing trap at 154 mph, and in solo trim recorded 176 mph.

It looked like being a fitting tribute to the ISO records meeting in October, for George was determined to go for a flying quarter average of 200 mph. As he was now 58 it would almost certainly be the last chance for him to break World records. At stake was the Chandy Trophy and £500, and the King of British record breakers looked to have a good chance if the conditions were favourable. Everyone agreed that George was the only man in the country capable of reaching the 200 mph average, but fate was against him. Through Saturday and Sunday 30 mph gusts of wind sadly blew George's chances away and there was nothing that any of us could do about it. George, philosophical as always, said: *You need perfect conditions to try for 200 mph, but these are just about the most dangerous conditions that it's possible to run in.*

The wind blew treacherously across the two-mile runway on the first day and not until the following day, in the face of a fierce crosswind, was George able to demonstrate the kind of form which could have taken him to the 200 mph record, had conditions been better. At one point the wind forced him to shut off as he was blown 10 feet off course. But in spite of the conditions he sped through the flying quarter at a staggering 190.315 mph. He touched 105 in first, 140 in second and was up to 180 in third on the run-in. On the return run he took the slab-sided dustbin fairing off Super Nero because it had been catching the severe gusts of wind, and he ran the bike 'naked' to reach 164 mph. It was not as fast as George had wanted, but in spite of the weather conditions 'the old man' didn't come away from

Attacking three-wheeler records at Elvington in 1970.

Elvington empty-handed. With sidecar attached, he took Super Nero to a new World and National record for the flying mile, completing the distance at a mean time of 28.074 seconds, which was 128.234 mph.

It was in 1970 that George made an enjoyable trip to Holland, having been invited there by a motor cycle club, who wanted his advice on the safety aspects of a drag racing course. Later a NSA team of riders including Antony Brown, with George as Captain, were invited over for a challenge match, which the British team won, Antony coming back from the meeting with three trophies.

It was also in 1970 that George had his first heart attack. He used to travel up the motorway in his Ford Cortina about every other week to collect spares and accessories from the Midlands factories for his shop. While driving back from Birmingham on the M1, pains in his chest were so bad that he was forced to pull onto the hard shoulder and rest for a while until they eased. After he had driven back to Stevenage, his wife Ada sent for the doctor and he was rushed to the Queen Elizabeth II Hospital at Welwyn Garden City and put on a heart machine. When he got out of hospital after six weeks it was with the realisation that his active racing and record breaking career was effectively at an end. At first he took it badly for his attack came as a complete surprise. His all-action life was over and he confessed to me that he felt cheated. He was also nervous of the future, perhaps for the very first time in his life, and his natural self-confidence had, for the moment, disappeared. He and I used to attend sprint meetings as we always had done, but now we were there only to watch and to chat to the competitors. There wasn't enough involvement in that for George, so he began to take more active interest in the racing careers of his sons. Antony and Graham were both attracted to road racing and George bought the elder boy, Antony, an Aermacchi, on which he entered for the Manx Grand Prix. He did quite well on it, but it was far too slow for the flying Yamahas. Later the Aermacchi was sold and George bought Antony a 350 cc Yamaha for the 1973 Manx meeting. He dismantled the engine and carried out a number of modifications. During practice week George was busy at the shop and couldn't get to the Isle of Man. Antony, on his own on the Island, had trouble because the bike kept seizing and holing pistons, but George showed the experienced touch when he arrived for race week and quickly put everything right. Tony was going well in the Junior Manx until he ran out of road on the Mountain and broke his thigh, though the bike wasn't even damaged. Antony was in and out of hospital for the next couple of years because of his injury and it really put paid to any more serious racing. As he got more involved with George's business, he didn't bother to race again.

Graham, George's younger son, now took over the Yamaha and started road racing. He showed so much interest that George bought him a more competitive TZ350 cc Yamaha and with this machine in 1978 he was doing practice laps for the Manx GP at around 100 mph. George was there, giving advice about the course, when and where to change gear, and how much it was necessary to reduce speed on certain corners. It was foul weather for the race — wind, rain and fog — but Graham must have been thinking about what his father had told him for he finished a very creditable 8th, an excellent position for his first race on the Isle of Man.

Other things also gave George pleasure during this period. He was particularly proud when Lord Montagu of Beaulieu asked him if he could have the loan of Super Nero Mark 1 for his world famous museum in Hampshire, and the legendary machine spent a couple of years on display there, before being brought back to Stevenage for a special show put on by the Vincent Owners Club. George also took both Nero and Super Nero to a big Vincent show in Giessen in West Germany. Our old colleague from Vincent days, Paul Richardson, did all the arranging because he could speak German fluently, and George, whose ill-health now prevented him from driving, travelled with Brian Chapman in his van with Brian's Vincent-powered Mighty Mouse and George's machines in the back. The Germans loved Nero and Super Nero and George could almost have named his own price. But he

Intensely patriotic, the Union Jack is well displayed as George rushes Super Nero ahead at Elvington 1970. *(M. Carling)*

told me when he came back that, for all the hours he and I had put in to make them record breakers, money could not buy his two most famous bikes and he would never sell them. It was a worrying time because George collapsed with another heart attack and spent the whole of the channel outward crossing in the ship's sick bay. He was urged to return on the next boat but wouldn't hear of it.

We were all quite worried about George's condition because by the summer of 1977 he had suffered two, if not three, heart attacks. It was also one summer evening in June, as my wife and daughter were preparing for our annual holiday in a couple of days' time, that I suffered a stroke. It happened as I dozed in a chair and I rolled out of it and onto the floor. At first my wife thought I was fooling, as I often played jokes, but this was no joke. I spent two weeks in hospital and had to learn to walk and use my left arm all over again. It was while I was in hospital that George and Ada went to the Isle of Man to watch the TT Races. On the Island George had yet another heart attack and spent some time in Nobels Hospital.

I was now 67, George 66, and with both of us out of hospital and home again in Stevenage we had to face the inevitable that the years take their toll and we were now getting older. George had come to terms with his retirement from record breaking and I thought it was now time for me to retire from full-time work. But I couldn't keep away from the shop and often used to find myself there chatting with George and Antony and keeping up to date with the new road models as they came in.

George took Ada to Germany in 1978 to attend the Vincent Rally of German owners at Niederbal, the two of them travelling with Mick Fraser. Again it was an extremely proud moment for George for he came back with a special plaque which had been presented to him. It was a large ceramic tile mounted on wood, the tile engraved with a picture of Super Nero, around which were all the signatures of the German Vincent Owners' Club members.

But time was rapidly running out. By the end of 1978 George had suffered seven heart attacks and he spent Christmas in nearby Lister Hospital in Stevenage. After Christmas he returned home and seemed to be making good, if slow, progress, but on February 27th, 1979, just five days after his 67th birthday, George had yet another heart attack. He was in bed and Ada had popped downstairs to answer the telephone. When she got back upstairs, a few minutes later, he was dead. The life of a unique character was at an end. Three weeks later Philip Vincent died at the age of 71 leaving, as far as I know, only myself and Phil Irving from the original team at Vincent — where it all began.

Chapter II

The Dream Denied

IN AN OLD BOX of press cuttings and photographs which George had gathered together as mementos of his life in motor cycles — and which I picked through in researching this book — were some special clippings from the *Daily Mirror* of Thursday, January 5th, 1967. They were all about Donald Campbell and the horrific crash on Lake Coniston in his jetboat Bluebird which had ended the speed-king's glamour life the day before.

George, were he able, would tell you that they were part of his private collection for a very special reason. For he regarded Campbell both as a friend and an inspiration. Though it would have been difficult to find two men more dissimilar in looks, they were in character and attitude very much alike. Both were stubborn, determined and persistent in the extreme. Both had that certain feel and flair for adventure. They shared a love of speed and a hunger for accomplishment. And both Donald Campbell and George Brown were driven by an intense patriotism which craved for the ultimate World Land Speed Record — on four wheels and two — to belong to Britain.

Campbell achieved that ambition for Great Britain in 1964 when he travelled at 403 mph at Lake Eyre in Australia to claim a new Land Speed Record. For George, it was a moment for reflection and despair, for had things turned out differently, he might well have been at Lake Eyre with Donald Campbell and, with luck, made it an eventful 'double' by claiming the ultimate motor cycle land speed record on Super Nero.

It wasn't for the lack of trying on George's part. Campbell had put a lot of his own personal fortune into his record breaking attempts. George was also willing to invest his own savings in an effort to secure the two-wheel world crown. Where the Campbell name, background and sense of history

— and the glamour of four wheels — were sufficient to enable Donald to go ahead with his plans, backing at the right level for George was never forthcoming. Around £10,000 would have done it, he told me once, and he was willing at that time to put in around £3,000 of his own money. But his voice was faint and hardly heard in a wilderness of comparative disinterest.

For six or seven long years George lived with the dream that one day he would attract enough sponsorship to make a realistic attempt on the World record a possibility. His proposition wasn't such a wild idea, if you now look back at the facts. In 1956 the official World record stood to the credit of Wilhelm Herz of Germany at 210 mph on a 499 cc NSU. Six years later, in 1962, the figure had only been improved by 14.5 mph. This record, by American Bill Johnson on a 649 cc unblown Triumph, was to stand 'officially' for a number of years.

Donald Campbell CBE discussing with George his forthcoming record attempt with his racing car Bluebird at Lake Ayre, Australia.

George with Super Nero and his two sons in 1972. Antony sits astride the Aermacchi which his father bought for him for Isle of Man racing and Graham demonstrates a good riding position on the trials bike. *(Post Echo)*

This was George's big chance. For when Bill Johnson was flashing over the Bonneville Salt Flats in September 1962 to set up his new World record of 224.5 mph, Super Nero was already a reality and by early the very next year, George was already turning in speeds approaching 200 mph on severely inhibiting short stretches of airfield tarmac in Britain. On the hard packed salt and wide open spaces of the Bonneville Flats, and with Super Nero tuned and equipped specifically for an out-right World record attempt, George must have stood a good chance of bringing the record back to Britain.

He tried desperately hard to get the trade interested. Companies he knew well, like Shell, Castrol, Avon, Champion and so on, were willing enough to provide free products, but what George needed was hard cash to cover the cost of taking Super Nero, himself and a small team over to America and there to be able to concentrate on the job without wondering if they might have to come back almost as soon as they arrived because they were running short of cash. At one stage George got all excited when Sir Alfred Owen seemed to get a bit interested, but nothing came of it. When hopes of going to Bonneville faded, his hopes rose yet again when Donald Campbell announced plans for his dramatic Australian attempt on the World record. In fact I believe it was Campbell's idea that George should try to muscle in on his show. It seemed reasonable enough, for if there was going to be a lot

In 1981 Antony, who now works in the Stevenage shop, with Super Nero and Cliff Brown with Nero.

The Stevenage premises as they are today, with the George Brown name proudly displayed.

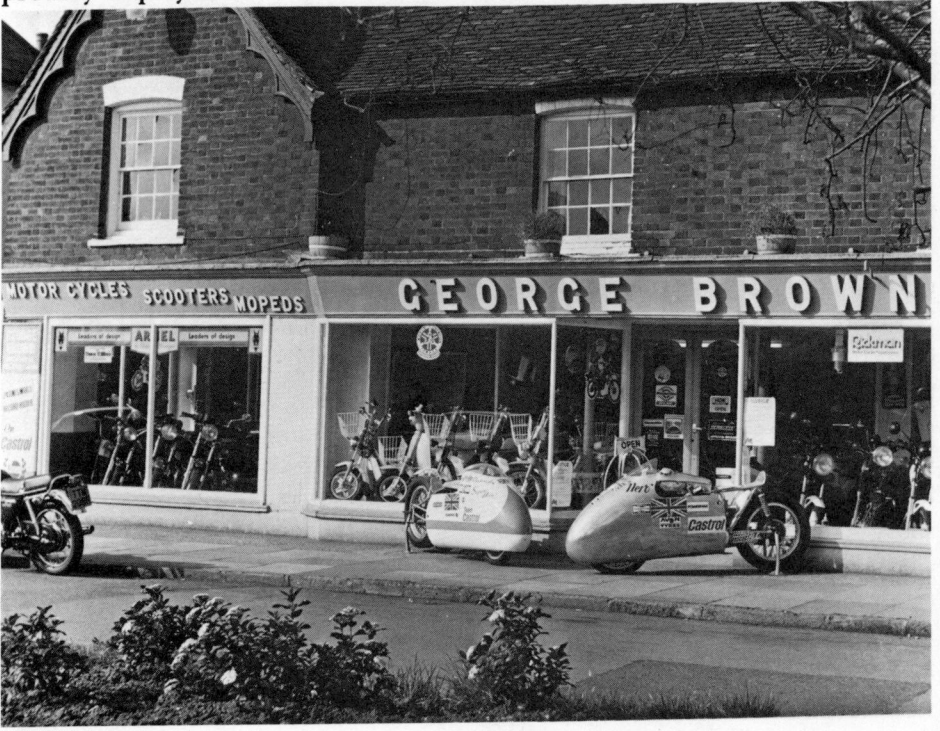

The author, Cliff Brown, with Nero, one of the record breaking machines on which he lavished so much care, time, skill and attention.

of sponsorship money about anyway, as there certainly was, then 'thumbing a lift' with Campbell might be the answer for George. The chance of an unprecedented 'double' might just capture the imagination . . . and give George the money he wanted. Moreover, he could have used Campbell's timing gear, stewards and other equipment.

Even the illustrious *Observer* newspaper was moved to go into print on George's behalf and in 1962 printed a long article which incorporated the following plea: *Somewhere, somehow, he (George) has to find the money that will enable him to spend three months in Australia tuning his machine to the prevailing conditions and experimenting. If he can provide that (some of the money), plus the acumen, ability and the guts to bring the record home to Britain, is it too much to hope that somewhere in this country is a backer who will make the project possible?*

But again nothing happened and while Donald Campbell was speeding to glory in Australia, and making headlines in all the world's most famous newspapers, George had to be content in taking Super Nero up and down grey and dull airfield runways in Britain, and competing for his share of column inches in *The Motor Cycle* and *Motor Cycle News*.

When George failed to get the backing he needed from Britain he turned reluctantly abroad. *The adventurous spirit of Britain is dead,* he said, complaining that other countries seemed to have little difficulty in backing attempts like his, but in Britain, as he put it, everyone seemed to be too tight-fisted. Almost in desperation, he tried to get support from Australia, even the Australian Government, when looking towards a link-up with Donald Campbell's four-wheel record attempt in Australia, but you could hardly expect another country to support what was a totally British attempt.

Nowadays the whole business of sponsorship is more professional and accepted within the world and there are firms who specialise in bringing together the money which commerce and industry set aside for sponsorship and the organisers of suitable events. But in the early and mid-1960s, there was far less gloss and sophistication about . . . and George went around shopping for the money himself. Who knows, in different times and by different means, George Brown might well have got the backing he needed and won that coveted World motor cycle record for Britain.

Typically, when George saw that the chance had gone, in the late 1960s, he accepted the reality of the situation and got on with other things. His motto was always to win . . . or bust. There were no half measures with George. He might not have achieved his ultimate ambition, but by God, he certainly made the world sit up and take notice of him.

Nowadays, into the 1980s, George's son Antony is running the Stevenage shop and business is booming. I often walk down there. Nero and Super Nero Mark I are still intact, exactly as George last raced them, and occasionally, in a quiet moment, I'll wander off and gaze at them . . . and think of what might have been if George had still been alive. But all the wishing in the world can't change things . . . and anyone who was closely involved with George for any significant period will have many wonderful memories for consolation.

Chapter 12

George the Man

GEORGE BROWN was a well respected name, not only in motor cycle sport, but with the customers who came to his Stevenage shop, among the members of his family, and with those who knew him as a friend or casual acquaintance. In his chosen way of life he was a man who did great things without fuss. Known for his outstanding success and for his capacity to out-sprint most of his sprinting contemporaries, recognition within the sport and his many triumphs never changed him. He remained quietly spoken, modest with a keen sense of humour, friendly and in many ways extremely sensitive to the needs of others, right to the end.

When it came to his beloved motor cycle sport he contributed more than might have been expected, finding reward enough in setting a new time or squeezing an improved performance from one of his famous machines. He became a successful businessman, but money never meant all that much to him. His record breaking must have cost him thousands of pounds. He told me at the time that his two Thurleigh efforts alone in 1960 cost him more than £1000 each, without the expense of the machines. If you were to calculate his time and mine, plus that of George's faithful team of supporters, in monetary terms, the figure would be astronomical.

He worked hard to build up and sustain his flourishing motor cycle business in Stevenage, being unstinting in time and work capacity. And he was equally generous when it came to directing considerable sums from the profits he made into his quest for record breaking honours.

Of course, in his own way he was egotistical. What successful man isn't? The desire for recognition and the excitement of success is what sparks-most of our ambitions. But George was always willing to give back more than he received. At one time when he was particularly busy and harassed he travelled to the Midlands on a Christmas goodwill mission, helping three hundred old-age pensioners and poor and needy children. Out of his own pocket he bought expensive timing equipment and presented it to the National Sprint Association. He never pushed sprinting down your throat, but if you showed any interest he would talk at length on his ideas and adventures. A devoted family man, he worshipped sons Antony and Graham — Graham being christened after George's road racing pal from the early years, Les Graham.

At the Avon works in 1949 and George and Gunga Din show off their trophies.

Chapter 12/139

George at Shelsley Walsh, where he was supreme no fewer than sixteen times. (Logan)

As a youngster George was quiet, long suffering and had a keen sense of humour. He was an excellent all-round sportsman and a cracking centre forward for the local village team; a great goal-scorer. When we both played for the old Vincent team, we used to say that if we could get the ball to George anywhere near the area he would give us a goal. Later he had a trial for Luton Town and at one point he thought seriously about an offer to become a professional soccer player. But by this time motor cycle sport had captured his imagination and was taking up too much of his time. He was also good at billiards and snooker. Though he smoked moderately, cigars in the later years, and had an occasional drink — Martinis being his favourite — he was by no means a hell raiser and his language, even when things went wrong and he was mad with someone, was temperate by racing standards.

During his most active days as a sprinter he was keen to keep physically fit and would go for long walks regularly and include bouts of running in his training. Even when he was at Vincents he would keep fit for those early TT rides by running from Stevenage to Baldock and back, a total of eight or nine miles.

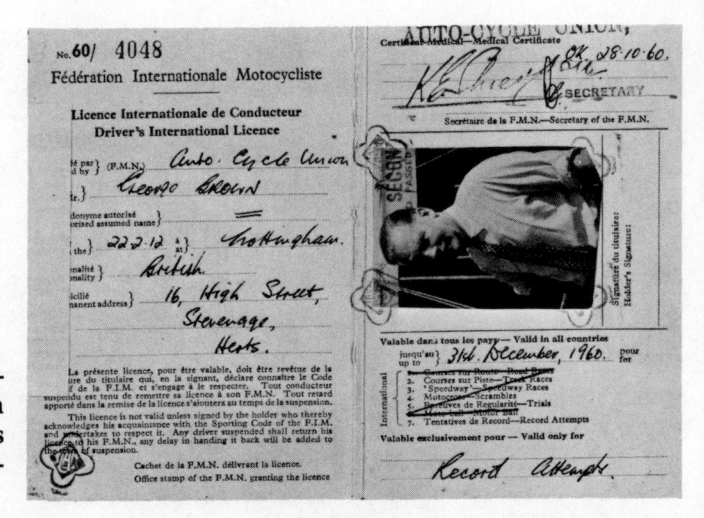

George's competition licence which initially curtailed his record breaking activities.

George had an abiding capacity for getting on well with almost anybody. He admired as early heroes riders like Les Graham and Geoffrey Duke and, later, John Surtees, and always thought a lot of people like Vic Willoughby, Steve Lancefield and Charlie Rous. He always responded well to any interest shown in his activities or his machines, even from his rivals. He was friendly with almost all of them, though for some reason I was never able to understand, the great London sprinter Alf Hagon seemed occasionally to stimulate a feeling of slight antagonism. I am sure it was totally illogical on George's part and merely an emotional reaction. Perhaps he saw Alf as a major rival and wouldn't therefore permit his natural instincts to be too charitable to him. Yet he wanted him in his team when he thought there was a chance of competing in America.

George wasn't the sort of person to be resentful or to build up feuds. Until the very end of his career he was always looking forward, rather than dwelling on past events. He very much admired the new breed of sprinters who followed him and would always give every bit of support and encouragement to those who worked long and hard doing their own bikes with hardly any sponsorship and for such small reward. He had the same dedication when he was working in the shop and I have seen him sit outside the Stevenage High Street premises patiently putting something right on a customer's machine or advising and helping on a problem. He was an able storyteller and his regular talks, which he illustrated with films, were very popular.

He was a fighter for what he thought was right, for himself as well as for others. You meet all sorts of people when you're running a business like

George's, and I've often watched, fascinated, while George handled certain difficult situations across the counter. If someone came in with a complaint, he could be exceptionally understanding and generous, but he reacted strongly if he had any suspicion that he was being taken for a ride. His early law training was useful when he had customers who threatened him with court action. It didn't happen often, but when it did he would study his law books and then deal with the situation confidently. It was no good anyone trying to intimidate George. That would make him mad and obstructionist more than anything.

During his peak years he lived for his record breaking and his motor cycle business. When he finally accepted the need to take things easy he gained a lot of pleasure of playing his collection of classical records and from mixing with riders. He continued to help the Stevenage Motor Cycle Club and never lost interest in the activities of the National Sprint Association and the Vincent Owners Club. Perpetual reminders with the Stevenage Club are the George Brown trophies. The first one, which I made for George in the early 1960s, incorporates a con rod used in Nero; the second, a piston once used in Super Nero. This was first competed for in the year George died. When Donald Campbell was killed in his attempt to secure the World's Water Speed Record on Coniston Water in 1967, George was proud to succeed him as President of the National Sprint Assocation. He had a great affection for Campbell and his sense of patriotism.

For me the saddest part of George's career was that he never gained what was for him, the ultimate ambition: the World's Land Speed Record on two wheels. Nor was he, I feel, given sufficient recognition from outside bodies. I know at one time Bemsee put his name foward for the Segrave Trophy, which is awarded annually 'to the British subject who accomplishes the most outstanding demonstration of the possibilities of transport by land, air or water'. But it would probably be at the time when this important trophy, which honours the memory of Sir Henry Segrave, was won by Donald Campbell or Captain George Eyston.

It's tragic that George's remarkable achievements received so little recognition. I remember him being bitterly disappointed after the celebrated Greenham Common meeting when he broke thirteen records. It really was a substantial success. Later he said: *After breaking 13 records I expected to come back to Stevenage to find the town band out and a civic reception.* But he rated just two column inches in a local paper.

When he died he still held seven National sprint records, though he had been retired for eight years, and seven National and one World record were still standing at the beginning of 1981.

The three large showcases which are to this day crammed with trophies also bear witness to an illustrious career.

British Motor Cycle Racing Club President, Sir Geoffrey Tuttle, hands over the coveted Les Graham Trophy to George Brown in 1968. *(Craine Roohe)*

Index

Abridge, 42, 70
Aermacchi, 128
AJS, machines, 9, 43, 60, 62, 63, 64, 74, 96, 173
AJS, team, 8, 36, 46
Allen, Johnny, 22
American Drag Association, 104
Ansty, 48
Applebee, Stan, 38
Ariel Arrow 250cc, 84, 85, 87, 90, 91, 92, 93, 108, 110
Armstrong, Reg, 62, 63
Ashwell, Ian, 96, 114
Auto-Cycle Union, 19, 20, 64, 84, 85, 91, 114, 125
Avon, 9, 16, 20, 76, 81, 82, 95, 133

Banbury, 74
Barnett, Syd, 44, 63
Barrett, Pat, 18, 20, 78, 81, 84, 85, 87, 91, 94, 96
Beaulieu, 128
Bell, Artie, 46
Bemsee, 8, 9, 99, 141
Bennett, Air Vice-Marshall, 59
BHN Group Trial, 42
Blackbushe, 106
Black Knight, 64
Black Lightning, 49, 52, 56, 59, 69, 94
Black Prince, 64
Black Shadow, 43, 57
Blackpool, 76, 94
Blandford, 48
Bluebird, 131
Bonneville Salt Falts, 55, 134
Bourne, Arthur, 38
Breeze, Arthur, 74

Brierley, Maurice, 16, 17, 18, 64, 80, 114
Brighton, 12, 70. 72, 74, 79, 80, 97, 99
Bristol, Goram Fair, 74
British Drag Association, 104
Brooklands, 8, 27, 33, 36, 39
Brough Superior, 30
Brown, Antony, 96, 104, 123, 124, 125, 126, 127, 128
Brown, Graham, 128

Cadwell Park, 9, 39, 40, 42
Cadwell Special, 39, 40, 42, 44, 45
Calthorpe, 27
Camathias, Florian, 16, 17, 78, 80
Campbell, Donald, 131, 133, 135, 136, 141
Campbell, Sir Malcolm, 93
Carr, John, 36
Castle Donington, 30
Castrol, 9, 133
Champion, 133
Chandy Trophy, 126
Chelveston, 11, 12, 22, 99, 100, 102, 106
Chester, 74
Church Lawford, 97
Clark, Bill, 34, 38
Clubmans TT, 38, 44, 45, 46
Cobb, John, 93
Cole, Len, 18, 78, 104
Coleman, Rod, 36, 62, 63
Comets, 8, 33, 36, 38, 40, 56
Coniston Lake, 131, 141
Cooper, Fred, 123
Cork, 97, 100
Coventry Eagle, 92
Craig, Joe, 8

Dance, G., 92
Daniel, Harold, 46
Daniels, John, 45
Davenport, M.E., 92
Davies, Howard, 34
Davis, Ted, 45
Dearden, Reg, 94, 95
Debden, 105, 107
Dixon, Freddie, 34
Donovan, D.R., 29
Doran, Bill, 44, 46
Duddington, Stan, 52, 72
Duke, Geoff, 40, 44, 62, 63, 66, 94, 108
Dunelt, 27, 29
Dunholme, 42, 46
Dunlop Trophy, 45
Duxford, 97, 102, 107, 108, 124

Elvington, 11, 12, 114, 123, 125, 126, 127
Eppynt, 9, 46, 56
Excelsior, 92
Eyre, Lake, 131

Farnanes Hill Climb, 98
Fernihough, Eric, 114
FIM (Federation Internationale Motorcycliste), 7, 10, 11, 12, 16, 18, 20, 84, 85, 91, 100, 107, 110, 112, 114, 120, 123, 124, 125
Folbigg Trophy, 39
Free, Rollie, 52, 55
Frend, Ted, 43, 44, 46
Frith, Freddie, 48

Gilera, 78, 86, 92
Gold Star Award, 8, 80, 99
Graham, Les, 9, 48, 63, 66, 138

Index

Gransden, 43, 52, 55, 56, 60, 74, 76, 81, 96
Greenham Common, 10, 11, 108, 110, 112, 114, 120
Greenwood, Owen, 123
Grey Flash, 57, 58
Gunga Din, 22, 43, 44, 45, 46, 48, 49, 52, 69

Haddenham, 44, 48
Hagon, Alf, 104, 123, 140
Hartlepool, 48
Hatton, Tim, 18, 81, 95, 96
Heath, Phil, 44
Heckle, Des, 123
Henne, Ernst, 94, 100
Hertz, Wilhelm, 132
Hinton, Harry, 44
Honda, 9, 96
Howdle, Peter, 120
HRD, 32, 33, 34, 92
Hutchinson 100, 42, 43

Impetus, 114
International Six Days Trial, 26, 34
Irving, Phil, 34, 36, 37, 38, 40, 42, 43, 44, 52, 55, 56, 96, 130
Isle of Man Sprint, 82
ISO, 14, 123, 126

JAP, 31, 34, 36
Jersey, 74, 79
Johnson, Bill, 132

Lancefield, Steve, 140
Lands End Trial, 38
Lawrence of Arabia, 30
Lawton, Syd, 62
Lazenby, Jack, 52, 57, 58
Le Vack, H., 92
Lockett, Johnny, 42
Lomas, Bill, 62, 63
Long Marston, 74, 78, 83

Mallory Park, 39
Manx Meeting, 128
Markham, Charles, 43, 52
Maudes Trophy, 27
McEwan, Tom, 63
McIver, Peter, 33, 36
Meteor, Comet, 33
Methamon, 16, 18
Milani, Alfredo, 16, 18, 78, 80, 83, 85, 86, 92
Milani, Gilberto, 16
Milhoux, Rene, 10
Montagu, Lord, 128

Monza, 92, 104
Motor Cycle Show, 16, 20, 31, 81
Motor Cycle, The, 38, 72, 81, 94, 102, 135
Motor Cycle News, 120, 135
Motor Cycle Sport, 98
Motor Cycle Weekly, 70
Motor Cycling, 38, 43, 52
Moule, Albert, 60
Munster Club, 98
MV Agusta, 16, 63, 66

Nero, 9, 16, 17, 18. 19, 20, 22, 60, 69, 70, 72, 74, 75, 76, 78, 79, 80, 81, 82, 83, 84, 85, 86, 87, 91, 92, 93, 94, 96, 97, 98, 104, 120, 126, 128, 136
New Hudson, 92
Norman, 58, 59
Norton, 8, 9, 28, 35, 36, 42, 46, 58, 60, 62, 63, 64, 66, 67, 68
NSA (National Sprint Association), 12, 14, 18, 78, 79, 80, 82, 96, 104, 105, 108, 114, 127, 141
NSU, 64, 76, 132

Observer, 135
OEC Temple JAP, 100
Old Warden, 30

Page, Val, 85
Pendine Sands, 70
Percival Aircraft, 37, 40
Phillips, Vic, 114
Picador, 57, 59, 80, 94, 96
Poddington, 108
Pontypool, 74, 93
Pope, Noel, 48
Potts, Joe, 9, 35, 60, 64
Prescott, 72

Radley Hill Climb, 76
RAF Motor Sport Association, 108
Raleigh, 8, 26, 27, 28, 29, 30, 31, 32
Ramsgate, 74, 79, 91, 94, 97, 99, 124
Redcar, 45
Rous, Charlie, 94, 97, 104, 140
Royal Enfield, 10, 27, 108, 110, 112, 120
Rubery-Owen, 21
Rudge, 34

Scarborough, 45
Segrave, Henry, 93
Segrave Trophy, 141
Shell, 133

Shelsley Walsh, 48, 70, 72, 74, 79, 92, 97, 98
Sherburn, 72
Shuttleworth, Richard, 30
Silver Star Award, 80. 99
Silverstone, 48
Snetterton, 82, 97
Stevenage Motor Cycle Club, 18, 125
Sunbeam, 92
Sunbeam Motor Cycle Club, 91, 94.
Super Nero, 9, 10, 11, 14, 21, 22, 75, 93, 95, 96, 97, 98, 99, 100, 102, 103, 104, 105, 106, 108, 123, 125, 126, 127, 128, 131, 132
Surtees, John, 8, 36, 58, 140
Swinderby, 107

TTs, 36, 56, 67, 68, 70, 93, 108, 129
TT, Junior, 9, 60, 64, 66
TT, Senior, 9, 63, 64, 66
Tadcaster, 91, 97
Terry, Jack, 74, 78, 91
Thurleigh, 15, 16, 17, 78, 84, 87, 92, 102, 103, 137
Triumph, 27, 104, 132
Tyler, Arthur, 36

Velocette 350 cc, 36, 62, 74
Vincent (company), 8, 9, 32, 33, 34, 35, 36, 37, 38, 40, 49, 56, 57, 58, 59, 60, 69, 78, 94
Vincent (machines), 9, 10, 11, 16, 38, 40, 42, 43, 44, 56, 60, 64, 72, 74, 76, 78, 87, 92, 94, 95, 96
Vincent Owners Club (Britain), 128
Vincent Owners Club (Germany), 130
Vincent, Philip, 8, 32, 33, 34, 36, 37, 38, 40, 43, 46, 52, 56, 57, 94, 130
Vines, F., 29
Vindian, 56

Walker, Graham, 38
Wellesbourne, 90, 96
West Ham Speedway, 40
Wheeler, Arthur, 62
Williams, Jack, 29, 36, 58
Willoughby, Vic, 70, 72, 81, 96, 140
Wiscombe Park, 97
Witchford, 76
Worters, J.S., 92
Wright, Joe, 99
Wright, Matt, 37, 38, 40

Yamaha, 128

Zenith 995cc, 27, 100